Praise

WOLF WOMAN: A SEAI

Justice Ryan, Aspiring female Indigenous family physician.

I cannot fathom a person in this world who would not benefit from reading Wolfe's memoir. I was unaware of how much I needed to know her story until I started reading it. Wolf Woman is a true beacon of hope and inspiration in what can seem like a dark and unfair world. Whether you have a similar story or not, you will leave this book with a new sense of empathy, perseverance and healing. I could barely take my eyes away from the pages as I cried, hoped, loved and ultimately grew with Beatrice through the eye-opening recount of her astounding life. From now on when I am faced with difficult times, I will remind myself, 'If Beatrice can do it, you and I can too.'

Aynsley Smith

This story shows the grit of life alongside the fire of resilience. It's a reflection of the inhumanity facing native women and the importance of hearing their stories and seeing them as worthy, brilliant beings. Thank you, Beatrice.

April Young, Survivor

An inspiring memoir, which is similar to my story, too. I identify because we both have given back to our communities. The drinking and using masked the real pain of our horrific lives. The victimization of prostitution became clear to me, despite my sick thinking that it was okay. To remember the pain of being marginalized hurts, yet I will persevere after reading this book.

Jackie Lynne, Co-Founder, Indigenous Women Against the Sex Industry (IWASI)

Wolfe's book is simultaneously heartbreaking, yet triumphant in its telling. The author writes of her painful beginnings as an unwanted, unloved Brown-skinned girl living within an abusive child welfare system to her life of chaos and survival on Western Canada's meanest streets. She has a profound spiritual experience which begins her healing process. In doing so, she says "yes" to life, and she becomes a powerful healing force for others. Her story, while painful to read at times, is full of hope, faith, and joy.

Julia Beazley, Director of Public Policy, The Evangelical Fellowship of Canada

Gripping and gritty, *Wolf Woman* is a story of abandonment, abuse, addiction and exploitation. But it is also a triumph of spirit, resilience, determination, profound grace and the fierceness of a mother's love. It is one woman's story, but Beatrice stands with and for far too many Indigenous girls and women failed by a society and a system that should honour and protect them.

Rev. Dr. David Hearn, President, The Christian and Missionary Alliance

If you have ever struggled with feeling inadequate, alone or rejected, feeling like you are simply surviving, fleeing the pain of this life – I encourage you to read this book. Wolfe's story shows how God can lift the most desperate life from the depths of despair to hope in Christ. Have you ever wished you had a hero to rescue you from your situation? If so, you need to read this story – Beatrice found help and you can too!

Barbara Gosse, CEO, Canadian Centre to End Human Trafficking

Wolfe provides an authentic and raw view into her very personal and shockingly traumatic young life, exposing the evil reality of predators, who act without remorse or fear of justice and thus detrimentally affect innocent lives forever. Her ultimate triumph, aided by those who see her strength, and soulful resilience, coupled with her recognition of the Creator's power, reflects a clear multiplier effect for what is right. Beatrice's path shaped a fearless community leader, from whom we can all learn.

Trisha Baptie, Founding Member & Community Engagement Coordinator, EVE (formerly Exploited Voices now Educating)

Wolfe is a resilient soul born into systemic oppression that affected her life daily. Those systems took her down for a while but did not take her out. This is a story of transformation and resilience of a woman who not only survived what was determined to kill her but who is now serving others who struggle under the same oppression and drawing attention to the systemic issues that must be dismantled. Serving a God bigger than all these issues, success is but a certainty.

WOLF WOMAN

A SEARCH FOR IDENTITY

BEATRICE WOLFE

WOLF WOMAN: *A Search for Identity*
Copyright © 2020 Beatrice Wolfe

ISBN 9780995083066 (Paperback Edition)
ISBN 9780995083073 (ebook Edition)

This memoir reflects the author's present recollections of experiences over time. Some names and characteristics have been changed, some events have been compressed, and some dialogue has been recreated.

Editing by Sherry Hinman
Front cover image by Laura Fauchon
Book Design by Kheyla Pehlke

Printed and bound in Canada
First printing October 2019

Published by Defend Dignity
Visit www.defenddignity.ca

DEDICATION

*For my Creator, who chose me, loved me
and watched over me.*

*And for my children, who inspired me to love myself
so I could love them more.*

Wounds from my childhood still run deep
A smell or a taste reminds me of my defeat
Trauma from my teens still haunts me today
As the memories constantly come into play

Life carried on abusing and being abused
If I had self-love this is not what I'd choose
The torment smothers me awake and in my sleep
This shit is honestly way too deep

As I work through my pain of days prior
Some days I still fall victim and call myself liar
Believing the lies surrounded by traumatic fears
Which are often comforted with my own tears

With every victory I grow stronger
until one day I will be free
And through my healing I will be able to see

myself

Smile without guilt
Laugh without embarrassment
Cry without shame
Hug without fear
Love without jealousy
Have righteous anger and work through it
Wake up not depressed
Talk without confusion
Believe in myself
Because in the end

I am victorious

#CreatorHasMe

ABANDONED

I WAS BORN in the fall of 1972, to Mary-Jane Wolfe from Muskowekwan First Nations in Saskatchewan. My father was a White man from Moose Jaw who disowned me when my parents broke up. Or so I am told. But I really don't know. I wonder about my father. Do I look like him? Are his eyes brown or blue? I wonder what he was like as a person. When I asked about my father, and the few things I'd heard about him were confirmed, I feared rejection so I never sought him out.

I don't know much about my mother, but I was told she was robbed of her childhood and heritage at a residential school, where she suffered much abuse, as did many in her generation. And like many in her generation, she turned to drinking. I was told she was always laughing and joking and that is probably where I got my sense of humour. And my curls — I got them from her. I saw a picture of her as a child, and she had tight curly hair just like mine. She was short, yet I am tall. I wonder what other characteristics I have of hers.

I was told my parents drank and fought a lot. I was also told that when my father "meaned" on my mom, even as short as she was, she put up a fight. That's probably where I get my spunk. These thoughts remain in my head because I will never be able to ask.

∞

I don't remember much about my early years with my biological family. I had four older siblings, Vince, Madeline, Ricky, and Patricia. When I asked my eldest brother what my family was like, he would say, "If you don't remember, I am not telling you." My sister Patti, who is a year older than me, told me we were left at home by ourselves on the reserve for days, with no food, no power, and no water. We were so hungry a couple times we ate dog food to survive.

When I was seven months old, Social Services removed me and my siblings from our home and put us into foster care. I went back and forth from my mom's home to foster care until, at age four, I was adopted into a White, middle-class home, without my siblings. I'm not sure what I missed most about my brothers and sisters. Being the baby of the family had given me extra perks. My brother Vince always made sure I was looked after first. I missed him.

I once dreamt I was in a long hallway and at the end I could see my mom. She was short and had curly brown hair, like mine. She knelt down and my brothers and sisters surrounded her, touching her and holding onto her with delight. They were so happy to be in her presence. But I felt fearful and did not want to go near her. The social worker and my soon-to-be adoptive mother, Jomaine, walked me towards my family. Once I got close enough, the worker gently pushed me toward my mom. I screamed and ran and grabbed on to my adoptive mom's leg. I remember feeling scared, but I'm not sure of what. Years later, when I asked Jomaine about the dream, she told me the dream was actually a memory. It saddens me to think that the last time I saw my mom, I was too scared to hug her, to feel her love. It haunts me to this day because I have so many questions that will never be answered.

∞

One of my first memories in my foster home is of me walking out of a bedroom and down a hall, rubbing my eyes. I could hear people talking at the end of the hall and could smell fried eggs. I saw a White man sitting at a round kitchen table. He turned to me. I stood there in my flannel cotton nighty, feeling shy. He must have sensed it and he motioned with his hand for me to go to him. I walked towards him and saw my new mom on my right, standing at the stove. The man grabbed me once I was near and put me on his knee and started bouncing me. I didn't know if I should be happy or scared. I wasn't sure what this attention was. Is this good or bad? Am I happy or sad? I believe he was Jomaine's ex-husband. I don't recall seeing him again.

∞

On my fifth birthday, I sat by the window on my hands so I would be less antsy. I wore a pretty yellow dress with flowers blossoming out of the fabric. I was not used to dressing so pretty, with my white frilly socks tucked over my black shoes that looked like taps. My short brown hair had every curl in place. It was hard to contain my excitement. I wanted to squeal in delight, but I was quiet. If I'd been able to tell time, I'd have known it was going really slowly.

I saw my siblings drive by. *Here they are. Oh my gosh!* I wanted to run out and hug them, but I looked at my adoptive mom and knew it was better to sit up tall with my legs crossed and hands on my knees. I heard my siblings chattering on the other side of the door. I was dying to talk to them.

The door opened. I forgot my properness and ran towards it, giving a scream of joy. My brother Vince was taller than I remembered and I felt like he deserved the biggest hug in the world. I squeezed him in pure delight. At first, my siblings stayed quiet while they looked around my new home. I examined their eyes and wondered if they knew how much I missed them. A tear escaped my eye. I wiped it away real fast and smiled. I whispered to myself, "I need you here with me. I need my protectors."

We sat down and looked shyly at each other. When the nervousness wore off, we began to play. I forgot where I was. I only knew that I was with the ones I loved most. I don't recall how my siblings looked, but I do recall the feeling of togetherness.

Who knows what led up to it. Maybe it was just part of his regular vocabulary, but I heard my brother say the "F" word. The word I now hate. It took my siblings away.

"Who said that?" My shoulders tensed up at the sound of my adoptive mom's voice. I bowed my head and shook uncontrollably. My siblings continued to play because they did not understand her tone of voice. I knew that tone.

She grabbed me from behind by my skinny arm and yanked me into the kitchen. I looked down.

"Who swore?"

"I did," I whispered. "I did." I did not want my brother to feel this fear. I glanced over at him, but he had no idea that I needed him to protect me. This time, I was protecting him. Tears streamed down my face and my heart broke. A whimpered cry escaped my lips. I turned and looked at the deep, dark cellar.

"There are snakes down there," Jomaine threatened.

The thought of them slithering around the basement floor made me cringe in fear.

"Please, don't put me down there." I could hear my siblings still laughing and playing. I cried softly, so they wouldn't hear. I didn't want to ruin the party. Jomaine bent down to my level, and her look pierced into my eyes.

"Who swore, then?"

I looked at her for a second. "I did," I whispered. More tears streamed down my face.

I'm wondering now, did I end up eating cake? My favourite is red velvet with cream cheese icing. Mmmmm. I wonder, did I get any presents? Did I play outside with my siblings? I don't know, because I don't remember what happened next. That was the last I saw of my four siblings until I became an adult. Heartbroken Beatrice. Worst fifth birthday party ever. I wonder if my siblings or my adoptive family remember this day as I do — a day that devastated me.

∞

I walked to school on my own. It was just one long block and it wasn't easy to get lost. One day, I tried to skip to school. I say tried because I had no rhythm. I was pretty awkward in most things I did. Hop up, hop down, one foot in front of the other. I stumbled and giggled to myself. I shook my head and my curls swished back and forth.

Why can't I skip to school? I looked down at the sidewalk. "Oops!" *I stepped on a crack. Gonna break my momma's back.* I had learned to amuse myself because I was a lonely child. I had no friends at school. Across the street, a girl lived in a big red brick house. Arrangements were made for me to play with her. I guess it's what we'd call a playdate now. I tried to play with her, but it felt forced. I wondered if she even liked me. I was awkward and loud and tried to learn how to play. Yet, depending on the setting, I was also sometimes quiet. But one thing is for sure: I was most definitely Brown.

As I entered the school's gates I saw several children, many blonde-haired and blue-eyed, laughing and playing on the swings. I loved to swing but the children didn't like to swing with me. As I walked through the dirt-filled playground, they pointed at me and snickered.

Stop it, I yelled, but only in my head to drown out the hateful comments. I kicked a rock, chased it a bit, and proceeded to the playground apparatus. No one played there so I climbed to the top, because after all, I was the queen of this castle. I swung upside down and stared at the bright blue sky. Birds chirped their encouraging songs and I tuned out the rest of the playground noise. I closed my eyes and hummed with the birds.

My peaceful moment was interrupted by a sharp pull on my short, curly hair.

"Hey, you stupid squaw! Get down from there." A boy glared up at me. "Why don't you go burn some wagons. We don't want you here!"

I swung back up and stared down at the light-brown-haired boy with the mushroom cut. I so desperately wanted to hop off the playground apparatus and pull his hair right back. He looked at his friends and laughed.

You boys are a bunch of meanies, I screamed in my head! *Gosh, I hate you all. Just leave me the hell alone for once.*

For a couple of years at school, I endured the abuse alone. I didn't have anyone to tell, maybe because I felt like no one would listen to me anyway. I peed the bed often and hated going to school. But I hated staying home too. I didn't fit in anywhere. Even though I was around many people, I was lonely.

∞

One day, not too long after my birthday, while Jomaine's teenage son, Frank, babysat, I stared at the TV blankly. I didn't know what show was on television but my ears paid attention. I looked at my foster brother, Blake, who was a year younger than me and whose crazy, bubbly personality made him a good friend. He had big blue eyes and his blond hair looked like it had been cut with a bowl. I poked him with my finger to see if he was really there. I played so much with my imagination that it was sometimes hard for me to comprehend what was real.

"Beatrice, come here."

The hair on the back of my neck stood up. I didn't want to go near Frank. I didn't like his games, and I hated his smell. He smelled like hate.

"Beatrice, come here," he said a little more softly, acting like everything was okay. I got up and looked at Blake. He was mesmerized by the TV and paid no attention to me. I put my head down and tiptoed towards Frank's voice. *Maybe he can't see me. Hopefully, he can't see me.* I saw his feet in the bathroom and he gestured for me to come in. I did what he said because he was so mean that I was afraid of him.

"Sit on the toilet. You have to pee," he said. I shook my head no. He pointed to the toilet.

I pulled down my pants and sat. My feet barely touched the floor. I heard him unzip his jeans. What an ugly sound. I kept my head down and eyes closed. He touched my private area and I cringed.

"Touch me," he said. I shook my head no, but he lifted my chin and pushed my face towards his groin. *Gross. Stop. I don't like this.* Someone banged on the door.

"Let me in. What are you doing?" Blake asked.

I felt sick. There was more banging on the door. Frank pushed me away and pulled up his pants. He smacked me on the head, knocking me off the toilet, and swore. He opened the door and pushed past Blake, swearing as he left. I was left lying on the floor, sobbing.

"What were you doing?" Blake asked.

I didn't answer as I slowly stood up, pulled up my underwear, and washed my hands with hot scalding water and lots of soap. I didn't like Frank's games. I didn't like him.

When I came out of the bathroom, Frank yelled, "Put your nose to the wall! Put your arms up." I raised my arms out to my sides and he placed books on my outstretched hands. It hurt to hold all that weight. I knew I wouldn't be able to hold them for long. My arms were too small and weak.

"I dare you to drop them!" he taunted. I screamed in agony in my head but shed no tears to prove it. He wasn't going to make me cry. I hated him!

∞

When I was six, I tried to show Blake how to have sex. I don't know if I knew what sex was, but Blake and I both had our pants down and we were walking towards each other as if we knew what to do.

Then Jomaine walked in and screamed, "Beatrice, what are you doing?"

I turned to look at her, confused, but then realized this was a bad game. She grabbed me, threw me in the hallway, and sped-walked to get a hanger. I began to sob. This was obviously a bad game that I'd been taught. I'm not absolutely sure who had taught it to me, so I will not point fingers.

I was beaten with the hanger and told, "You're a dirty little kid." But nobody thought to ask where I had learned to perform a sexual act. Instead, I just accumulated more shame. You would never have known I was beaten because she was an expert in hiding my wounds. She would hit me on the back of my head with objects. She was very good at not bruising my face or my body, but I sure felt the effects afterward.

∞

One day, I lay down in the living room, wrapped in my blankie and planning to nap. A man yelled from the TV, his voice piercing my ears. It was too loud. Televangelist Jimmy Swaggart blasted on the television. All I could hear was mumble jumble.

"Close your eyes and sleep," Jomaine scolded as I curled up in my blanket, squeezing my brown eyes tight. I peeked at her, iron in hand at her ironing table. With the preacher blasting, how could I rest?

Jomaine never went to church except on special occasions like Easter and Christmas. I hated those times because I had to sit on my hands so I wouldn't touch anything, a difficult feat for a six-year-old child. Most Sunday mornings, Jomaine's friend Jean would pick Blake and me up in her big brown van. She had three adopted sons. That's probably why she was friends with Jomaine. Jean was a bigger lady and she always had a sour look on her face. Blake and I would stand by the door of our house and peek out the window to make sure she did not have to wait for us. I would be dressed in my Sunday best, carrying a Bible. As soon as we saw her van turn the corner, we sped-walked out to her van because we were not allowed to run to the city street.

Jean was not the type of person you'd want to sit and talk to, but then again, it might just be that she intimidated me. When the van stopped, we jumped in fast and she would usually be scolding her kids. I kept my mouth shut and my head down. It was none of my business and at least I was out of the house for a few hours.

On our way to church, we usually stopped to pick up Ruth, an elderly lady who sported tight, short, permed hair. Ruth was the light of my life. I would watch her walk towards the car ever so slowly. I was ready to greet her every time. She had a smile for me and looked at me in the eyes and said, "Good morning, Beatrice."

I would smile and even blush as she made me feel so loved inside. For her, I would let my guard down, with a big, "Hello!" I always sat beside her on the way to church.

After Frank moved out, Ruth would babysit us when Jomaine went out in the evenings. Thank God *Frank* didn't babysit anymore. I loved when she came over.

One evening when Ruth was caring for us, I cried because my growing pains were so bad. When my legs cramped up, I handled it by crying to myself. But this time Ruth heard me and came into my room to ask if I was okay. I told her what was going on and she asked if she could massage my legs.

She hummed and said, "Don't cry. It'll be okay."

I felt her care. I knew she loved me because she'd told me once. I remember this moment so well because it was the first time I could recall hearing those words with genuine care.

One Sunday we didn't go down Ruth's street. I asked Jean why. She told me Ruth was sick and probably would not come to church anymore. I gasped and covered my mouth.

As we made our way to church in Jean's van that day, I felt an emptiness when I looked at where Ruth was supposed to sit. *Will it ever be her seat again? No it won't.* I would never see Ruth again, but I will always remember the gentleness of her soul.

∞

Sunday school was just an escape for me. I never really got who this Jesus character was because I was too busy fidgeting and wondering what we would have for snack. I always asked to use the washroom, and I would wander the halls until someone found me. The Sunday school teachers would chase me back to class, and I would giggle and run because nobody ever told on me. Except for this one time.

Thinking back, I'm not too sure how it happened, but I recall someone saying they saw me steal money from the offering plate. I hadn't, but I knew that if this got back to Jomaine, I would be doomed. This experience didn't help how I felt about church. If anything, all this misplaced accusation turned me right off of it. I started to hate going there more and more. I always felt that eyes were staring at me. I was not allowed to use the washroom alone anymore. By the time I turned nine, I hated church and I hated God, the God they said loved me so much. I truly did not see this love everyone talked about.

∞

Grade 4 was a fun year. That was the year my new best friend, Anita, came to my school. Her family was all Brown-skinned like me. We both had a crush on Lindsay. He was cute and funny. He made me laugh, especially when he squinted his big blue eyes and yelled, "You can't catch me!"

One day, we were wearing our rubber boots and waiting for the recess bell to ring. We were puddle jumping and one of us was going to catch Lindsay. Today it would be me. When the bell rang, we all raced out the door. I laughed, and Anita and I ran as fast as we could. We weren't sure what we were going to do if we caught Lindsay. Nonetheless, we chased him until the bell rang to go back in. Our red rubber boots were covered in mud — mud up my pant leg. *Oops, I'm gonna be in trouble.* But it didn't matter. Today had been a good day. Anita and I skipped to our class. She was my absolute best friend.

∞

My yellow-painted room greeted my eyes as I awoke. I sat up in my bed, ready to take on the day. I had my bed and a dresser but no toys. I sat on the edge of my bed and swung my legs back and forth, humming a little tune, safe alone and waiting to be let out of my room. I didn't want to pee in the closet again.

I heard talking on the other side of the door. Freedom awaited me soon. I heard Jomaine unlock the door, and I lay down quick. I didn't want her to know I was awake. The door opened and I heard her walk away. I quickly jumped up and ran to the bathroom. How do you spell relief? *PEE.*

Back in my room, I made my bed and smoothed the covers until there was not a wrinkle in sight. I changed into my clothes, folded my cotton nightie, and tucked it under my pillow. I ran my fingers through my short curly hair. Man, I looked like a boy. I wished my hair was long and blonde like my beautiful adoptive sister, Mary. She had pretty blue eyes, a gorgeous smile, and a heart of gold. I loved her because she always stuck up for me. I wished she still lived here. I missed her when she moved away and got married. Back when Mary and I were roommates, Jomaine never locked the door. We never had a clean room, probably because she had lots of stuff, but we never got in trouble for it.

When I looked around my room, I saw that I had only one thing on my dresser, a porcelain figurine. She had bright skin; blonde, shoulder-length hair; a beautiful face; and a flowy yellow dress. She looked nothing like me. She looked like my adoptive sister. The figurine, like everything around me, was White, and I was not. She held the number ten in her tiny porcelain hands. That was my age and my reminder. No birthday parties since my fifth. None that I remember, anyways. Unless my memory is playing a mean joke on me and I've actually had the most amazing, fun, and laughter-filled birthdays every year. But I doubt that.

One hot summer morning, I sat under a tree in the backyard while the gentle breeze touched my skin. One of my escapes from reality was a binder full of poems and a story that I was writing. My story was about a young beautiful Brown princess the same age as me, 10 years old. She was lonely and sad but she had hope — hope to be rescued by someone or something. I wrote hard, sharpening my pencil and vigorously erasing, making sure to capture the right words. I closed my eyes and smiled and daydreamt about what to write next. Would a prince save me…? No. Would a dragon come rescue me and fly me to a safe place on a little island…? My thoughts were interrupted.

"What are you doing?" Jomaine yelled from the open screen door.

"Nothing, just writing."

"You and that stupid binder. What's in there? You're wasting your time. Nothing good is going to come from it."

I looked at her and saw that her mouth was still moving but I couldn't hear a thing. I felt an anger I couldn't control. I stood up, binder in hand, walked to the garbage can and threw it in as hard as I could, listening to it bounce at the end of its fall. I threw it so hard, papers flew out of the binder. I looked at Jomaine, a feeling of defeat washing over me. *Why does she hate me?* I walked to the tree and sat where nobody could see me and sobbed. I mourned about not finishing my story. Eventually, my anger turned into sadness.

∞

I checked my room, checked my clothes, checked my hair. *Am I good enough to start the day? Well, it's gonna have to be good enough because it's all I have.* It seemed as though I was always in trouble, always doing something wrong. Was I a completely rotten kid who deserved to feel like she was a burden to her family?

I was often blamed for my brothers' doings. If they stole something from the fridge, I would get blamed. How fair was that? I started acting out. If I was going to get blamed for everything wrong that happened in the house, well, I figured I might as well start doing those things. I was going to enjoy that banana I was forbidden to have! Yes, I was going to steal it and eat it, and you better believe I was going to enjoy it. It wasn't like I fit in anywhere, anyways. I was still an outsider. No matter how hard I tried to impress those around me, my efforts went unnoticed, so why try?

One afternoon when I got home from school, Jomaine called me inside. I glanced in her direction. She was mad. My heart skipped beats. I hated getting in trouble.

The only loving touch I received was after I was beaten. Jomaine would hug me and say, "That hurt me more than it hurt you." I hated that saying. Many nights, I went to bed right after my beatings and stayed in my room, crying and listening to the children outside laugh and play, too scared to look out the window at them for fear I would be caught.

I was in my room again, screaming into my pillow, loud in my head but quiet to the world. Again, bed without supper. What the hell did I do wrong this time? Children played outside. I heard the skipping rope hit the pavement. They giggled with satisfaction. Did I dare stand on my bed, peek out the window and take a glimpse of where I wanted to be? My body hurt from crying.

I heard her as she walked outside my door. She stopped to listen. I decided to wail. I wanted her to hear the pain in my cry. I didn't care if I would get hit. I wanted to play outside. I wanted to stop being in trouble. I wanted a mommy's hug or to be told, "You've done a good job."

I considered my life. Father leaves. Mother leaves. Brothers and sisters too. Who am I? Where do I belong? Alone? Dead? I wanted to die. I always did. I was so tired of being left out. I was so tired of feeling like I was always getting in shit. For once, just for once, couldn't someone actually love me? Say it and not because you feel bad for giving me a lickin'. Say it because you truly mean it. I was tired of being different. I was tired of feeling alone. I was tired of feeling like I was not doing anything right. I just wanted someone to hold me and comfort me. Someone to say, "Hey! You're a good girl," or "Hey! You're doing an awesome job." Something encouraging, just once!

I cried harder. Loneliness turned to bitter anger. When she hit me, it felt good because I was in control of my tears. But in the bedroom alone, my scream into my pillow was anguished. The tears controlled me.

Love me, hold me, want me, need me — that was all I wanted. I held my knees tight, in a fetal position, and rocked myself to sleep. I learned I could look after myself and, in that, there was a sad satisfaction.

In the morning, I awoke hungry to a dark and mean world. And in order to survive in it, I had to adjust to it if I was going to make it through another day.

∞

I hated myself, especially the colour of my skin. One night, I sat in the tub and scrubbed my skin hard with a face cloth until I thought I was "White." At school I was a class clown, but as I walked home the loneliness set it. When I entered my house with head bowed, I was never greeted with a, "Hello my girl, how was your day?" If I was ever greeted, it was with a look of disgust or a smack to the head. You don't want to know how many times I was smacked around and sent to my room for somebody else's actions. And the adults in my life wondered why I acted out?

∞

One day at school, my teacher gave me a tree to take home to plant. I walked home, hoping that Jomaine would let me plant it. I put the tree on the side of the house and walked inside. "I'm home," I said as part of my daily ritual. Usually, I took off my school clothes and played in the backyard till supper. On that day, I changed my clothes, stood in the hall, and braved up the courage to interrupt Jomaine's soap opera.

"Mom?"

She looked at me, surprised. "What do you want?"

"I was given a tree at school. The teacher said we could plant it at home. Can we?"

She sat there silently for what seemed like an eternity, then finally said, "Yes."

I was blown back by her words. Feeling giddy inside, I smiled and said, "OK."

"Go outside and get the shovel. We'll find a place to dig the hole."

I practically ran outside, but there was no running in the house. Outside, I looked at the big backyard to see where the tree would fit best. Once planted, I stood in the yard watering the tree and I glanced at Jomaine. She stood, hands on hips. It seemed she was admiring our work.

"Good job," she said. My heart felt happy. I liked this mom.

∞

Jomaine was a well-respected woman in her community. People who knew her from a distance admired and respected her because she fostered children with severe disabilities and she ran a home daycare. Sometimes it seemed like there were hordes of kids everywhere, and I helped watch these children in the summers during the day.

I wondered to myself why Jomaine adopted me. I called myself "the Indian slave" because I tended to the foster children who were my age and younger. I was forced to play with them and I didn't want to. I wanted to play with my friend.

I went outside not only with the foster kids, but also with the daycare kids. Kids, kids, everywhere. It was a tad annoying. It wasn't like I got paid to watch them. Why did I have to stay outside in the blistering heat with them? How would their parents like it if they knew that Jomaine was over at my sister Mary's house down the street, leaving me home to watch them. Don't think anyone would appreciate that, I tell you. I did all this, always trying to earn her love, always wanting Jomaine to love me or tend to me once in a while.

∞

Jomaine got me a job delivering flyers, but I got sick of her taking all my flyer money. I was the one who delivered the flyers, why didn't I get to keep the money? One afternoon, when I was supposed to be out delivering flyers, I went into a nice grassy back alley and took all 120 flyers out of the bag, left them in the alley, and lay down. I chewed on grass and stared up at the blue, cloudy sky.

I did this two more times before Jomaine confronted me.

"Why have you been dumping the flyers in the alley?"

I didn't answer.

"You know what people are going to think?"

I didn't answer.

"Answer me!" she screamed in my ear.

"I . . . don't . . . know. . . " My famous words nowadays. I knew she hated when I said them, which is why I did. I wasn't going to say, "You know, I got tired of you being an asshole so I decided to be an asshole back." No way! Saying "I don't know" would usually shut down the conversation and bring out the ass-whipping and room time. And then it would be over for the night.

∞

As I got older, church became boring, mostly because I found everyone so hypocritical – in *and* out of the church. Jean yelled at us all the way to church, but as soon as we hit the church parking lot, she was all smiles. Jomaine walked into church on Easter after not being there for months and everyone greeted her like she was the best person in the world. Meanwhile, back at home, she was making my life miserable.

On Wednesday evenings, I attended a church program called Pioneer Girls. I hung out with the "shit disturbers" because the reality was I didn't care about this church, this life, and most definitely this mean God who I'd felt pressured and guilted into knowing. Who were the people in the church to judge? They didn't know what I was going through. They looked at me as an outsider so I might as well act that way. If this Jesus character was as loving as they said he was, why did he let me live in such misery?

∞

The day I was told my mom died is so vivid in my mind. I was done with this so-called life. I hated myself and my environment. I hated everything. I could taste death as it danced in my head. I wanted that ultimate escape.

I was twelve, and Jomaine called me to come and sit beside her, outside on a bench. It was summertime and it was a beautiful day. I found it odd that she called me over because most of the time I was not allowed near her, or even in the same room as her. I would either be in the basement, where I ate supper alone, or outside in 40 below weather, where I stood in the backyard, freezing for hours, alone. I was not allowed in the living room, or to eat with the family, and at night time I was locked in my room for the "safekeeping" of the house.

When I sat down, Jomaine looked at me and said, "Your mom is dead." When she spit those words out, I looked at her. I thought maybe she was just saying that.

"Really?" I asked.

She looked at me with no emotion — well maybe some emotion, maybe resentment that I would even question her. "Does this upset you?" she asked. "Your mother didn't love you. She didn't even want you."

I put my head down and said, "It doesn't bother me." But that was far from the truth. A piece of me broke that day. A piece of my heart, my hope, my life, shattered. In my dreams, I would be all alone but my biological mom would come and rescue me. She would hold me in her arms and tell me how sorry she felt and say it had all been a mistake. She'd say she loved me, and my brothers and sisters and I would be happy forever. But now it was clear that dream would never happen.

That night, like many other nights, I cried myself to sleep. But this time it was different. This time it hurt *soooo* much. This time I couldn't breathe. How could I continue to live? How would I make it through the night? I just wanted to die.

I continued to act out at school and I acted out at home. I didn't care anymore. I remember going to the mall with my friend, and she had money but I didn't. She would buy stuff while I watched. I would touch the things I wanted and wish for them.

"If you want it, just take it," she said. "Just don't get caught."

I saw these stickers I wanted to add to my collection. I looked around before shoving them into my pocket. That was not hard, but of course, I got over-confident and started filling up my pockets.

When we were ready to walk out of the store, a security guard grabbed my arm. "Come with me."

Fear set in as the guards escorted me away from my friend. They took me to a room and told me to empty my pockets. Then I sat there until the police came. There was a woman cop and a man. My palms began to sweat. Up until then, I had never encountered police officers.

"How old are you?" the woman police officer asked.

"Twelve," I said, terrified.

"You realize we have to take you home to your parents' house."

I felt like I was going to throw up. "Oh, please no!" I begged.

I must have looked pale with fear because she acted softer towards me, especially in her tone. They escorted me to their police car and put me in the back seat.

"Where do you live?"

I wouldn't tell them. We sat there for a long time. I sobbed in the backseat. "You don't understand. You can't take me home."

"Why? Will something happen to you?"

"No," I sobbed, "but please, please, I promise not to do it again." I cried uncontrollably, and the officers spoke quietly in the front seat. I never said anything bad about Jomaine, but they must have heard my fear and pitied me. They ended up dropping me off at the end of my block. I ran home and never spoke about what happened to anyone and I never stole again. Well, at least not from the store as a child.

I did continue to rebel quietly and stole little bits of change here and there to buy one-cent candy from the store. I stole an apple because, well, when I was hungry I couldn't just *have* a snack; I had to steal it. When the kids made me angry at school, I would take their lunches from their lockers and throw them in the garbage. I threw their rubber boots out into the rain. I talked back to the teachers. I failed Grade 6 because of my attitude.

There were weekends when I wasn't grounded and could hang out at Anita's house. We would laugh and run through the park attached to her backyard. We'd lie in the grass, staring up at the sky, and dream about what we would do when we grew up. I wanted to be a singer, so we would practice, using her ghetto blaster. I would sing *Heaven*, by

Bryan Adams, as best as my vocals would allow me, and she would record it, play it back, and critique me. We laughed when I sang too high and she would say, "Cut! Do it again," and we'd take turns singing all afternoon.

∞

In my eyes, I wasn't a terrible child. I was merely adjusting to my environment and how I was being treated. One day, at thirteen years old, I came home from school to find out I must have done something to set Jomaine off once more. Or did Frank steal her earrings again? Did he put them on my bed to frame me? Whatever the case, she was angry and I didn't even have my shoes off before she tore a strip off me. I never talked back to her, argued, looked her in the eyes, or did anything to disrespect her. I would put my hands behind my back and squeeze them together until they turned white from my tight grip, just so I would not react. Just so she would not win. Finally, I would break down and a tear would escape my eye. I would be so mad at myself, but not this time.

By this time, I was taller than her and more athletic. I had joined every team in my school and was always one of the primary players. Jomaine would never know that because she never came to any of my games — that would have meant she had taken an interest in me. This particular afternoon, she kept hitting me with a broom and I couldn't take it anymore. I grabbed the broom from her and threw it down the stairs. I looked directly in her eyes, pushed her, and said, "You will never hit me again."

I immediately regretted it. I felt a sense of shame. I knew something was about to change. I felt it in the air. I heard it in her voice as she sobbed quietly on the phone. I heard it in the tone, later, when she and the social worker taunted my ears with their whispers that were just quiet enough that even though I strained to hear, everything was muffled.

But I most definitely felt it when I saw my packed suitcase at the door. Maybe it was a sense of sadness, or maybe it was fear, when Jomaine spoke those words that would shift my whole being. "You're leaving."

The next day, she drove me to a Native girls' home. That day will always be a wonder. If I had just let her hit me, would I have been forced to leave? On the drive to the Native girls' home, I bawled my eyes out, begging her not to reject me.

"Please don't send me there! I promise I will be good." I was so scared. I looked at her and she just kept on driving, stone-cold faced. I was losing something. I didn't know then, but another piece of me was breaking. This was the second time a family did not care enough to look after me anymore. I was just an object, and my feelings were not an issue, because if they had cared for or loved me, they would never have given up on me. I felt like garbage, thrown away for the second time.

∞

We pulled up to the two-story house. I wiped my eyes, now swollen red from crying. This was my fate. I was not going home ever again. Why was I crying? Why did I care? My insides hurt so much. *Please don't let this be real.* I sat and took a deep breath. My heart pounded so hard I could hear it. I was so scared.

Jomaine wiped her own tears away. *Why are* you *crying? You can stop this*. But I wasn't going to try to reason with her. She had made up her mind.

I held my suitcase and wiped the last of my heartfelt tears. I would never ever cry for her again. *You don't want me. Well, I don't want you either.* We stood at the door and she rang the doorbell. The door opened and we were greeted by a young, Brown-skinned woman. *She must work here.* She smiled and asked us to come in. The living area was where the offices were. She guided me to sit down on the chair and wait for her while she and Jomaine talked behind closed doors. I sat there in silence. There was no one else in the house. The other girls must have been in school. I waited patiently.

The door opened after what seemed like an eternity and Jomaine walked out, head down. No hug. No "See you later." Just walked out of my life.

SEARCH FOR IDENTITY

"Do you want something to drink?" the worker asked.

I shook my head no and just sat there. She went into the office and came out a few minutes later.

"Beatrice, come here. I have a few questions for you."

I sat there, tired as heck. I'd been through so many emotions the last few days. I was in no mood to talk. She asked me some questions. I nodded yes, shook my head no, and once in a while I'd say, "I don't know." I was too tired to care.

"I'll get your room ready. I'll be right back."

I sat there unable to grasp what was going on. She walked away and left me there, alone, lost, confused . . . numb. On her desk, I noticed there was a file with my name on it in big bold letters. I looked behind me and listened. She wasn't there. My curiosity overtook me. I flipped open the file folder. The first thing I saw was a paper with information previously unknown to me: "Beatrice Wallace's birth name is Wolfe and her mother is Mary-Jane Wolfe." *What the heck. How do I process this? What am I supposed to do with this information? This is too much for one day. Please stop it.* I just wanted to sleep. I closed the file and became completely unaware of my surroundings.

"Beatrice, come with me."

I jumped up, obediently grabbed my suitcase and followed her. We walked through the kitchen, past a long table. We proceeded upstairs, passing some other rooms on the way. She pointed out the bathroom we all shared and opened the door to my room. It had a single bed in the corner and a small dresser — it actually resembled my previous room in its simplicity.

"This is your room. You must be tired. Do you want some time to settle in?"

I nodded yes.

She walked to the door and said, "The girls will be home from school in a bit. Get settled and come down when you're ready." She left and closed the door.

I lay on the bed in my favourite rolled-up position, held my legs, and rocked myself to sleep.

∞

I heard a knock on the door and someone on the other side yelled, "It's supper time."

I automatically jumped up. I looked around, forgetting where I was. I just about started crying again, but I couldn't cry right now. I shook it off, walked solemnly to the washroom, washed up, and headed downstairs.

I was nervous as I walked down the stairs. I did not know how to act. *What do I say? Will they like me?*

I turned around the corner and saw a table with four Brown girls seated around it. There was an open spot for me, and one of the staff, Laura, proceeded to introduce me. I was numb. I didn't know how to feel. There was a girl who made her presence known. She looked at me as I sat and snickered at me. Then she looked at the other girls and laughed.

"Fresh meat," she said.

I sat down and tried not to look nervous. I grabbed my plate full of food that was already waiting for me. I don't remember how it came out or why I said it, but I told one of the girls something at the table and I used the word "bitch." What a mistake.

Justine, a girl who was the leader in the house, looked at me and squinted, her eyes gunning me off.

"You will never refer to any of us as bitches," she said. "The only bitch here is you." She got up to leave the table and the other three girls left with her.

Laura looked at me. "Just watch how you talk to her and you'll be okay," she said. She got up. "It looks like you're on dishes tonight." She left the room. I gobbled my food down and gathered the dishes.

As soon I started washing them, Justine walked up behind me, kicked my calf and said, "Welcome, bitch." She walked to the office. I held in my fear and tears, finished up the dishes, and walked quietly up to my room. I never wanted to leave my room again. I hated my life. I just wished to die.

∞

Days turned into weeks, and being in this home didn't get any easier. In the summer, we had a lot of free time. I would be going back to my school to finish Grade 8 in the fall and truthfully, I missed it. At my home, I was desperately trying to adjust. How does a person get accustomed to always feeling frightened and not being accepted? *Heck, I should be used to this.* I had experienced it all my life.

On one particular day, we were in the basement of the girls' home where we just hung out and listened to music. Here, I could join in conversation and not be ridiculed. We watched music videos.

"Do you know how to fight?" Justine asked.

"I don't like to fight," I said.

She called one of the shorter girls over. "Show me how you fight."

Dang it, I didn't want to fight. I'd been in one fight in my life and it was the fakest fight in the world. My best friend, Anita, back in Grade 6 wasn't liked at school because she was Brown like me. As a way to fit in, I said I would pretend to fight one girl and the other girl would fight my friend. My friend gave her a good old beating. I hit the girl I was fighting, knocked her down, and sat on her.

Everyone was yelling, "Hit her, hit her!" But I couldn't. I was so happy when that fight was over. I couldn't explain that I hated fighting. I hated hitting people. That was just not me.

"Come on. It doesn't mean anything. We're just playing," Justine said.

I stood up to leave and the rest of them surrounded me.

"Hit her," Justine yelled. The girl punched me in the face. I was stunned but it didn't hurt me. I grabbed my face in shock and pushed my way through the other girls.

"I'm not playing this stupid game," I said. I ran upstairs and went to my room. I didn't feel a thing. It didn't hurt my feelings — didn't make me mad or sad. I didn't care. What the hell was there to care about?

Another day, the girls and I were outside on the front lawn, suntanning. Haha, such a concept. We didn't need to get darker, although I had much lighter skin colour than the other girls.

"Do you think you're pretty?" one of the girls asked.

"No," I said and laughed.

"Well you're the prettiest of our group," Justine said. "The boys are always looking at you. Don't you see that?"

To be completely honest, I hadn't seen it. I didn't wear makeup, didn't care to fix my hair, seriously didn't give a crap how I looked.

"Let's give her some hickeys," one girl said. They laughed.

"You want some hickeys, Beatrice?" another girl asked. I scrambled to get up, but one girl grabbed me and I tripped. One girl sat on my feet, two held my arms, and another gave me hickeys all around my neck. Finally, they let me go.

"What the hell is wrong with you guys?" I yelled.

"Holy, we were just playing," one of them said. They snickered.

I ran into the house and looked at my neck in the mirror. Hickeys from one side to the next. What a frickin' joke.

I felt rejected by all humankind. First, I'd been denied at a young age by my Indigenous biological family. Then, I'd been denied by the White community and now again by First Nations. As far as I knew, I was half Native and half White, and they both rejected me. *Where do I fit in? Why am I not wanted by anyone?*

The girls at the group home told me I was an apple — brown on the outside and white on the inside.

I just did not want to live. I would have killed myself long before that, but someone once told me that when I died I would burn in hell because of who I was. I was also told if a person killed themselves they would burn in hell for eternity. Oh, how I wanted to die, but I didn't want to burn in hell, so I suffered through my young life. Every morning I woke up dreading the day. I didn't want to eat anymore. I didn't want to speak anymore. I just wanted to sleep my life away.

∞

A new girl, Christina, came to the house and the bullying was mostly redirected towards her. I knew how she felt. Christina was pale-skinned, tall, and pretty. She seemed nice. I didn't see her much because she was always hiding in her room. Her room was beside mine and I'm not sure, but I think I heard her crying. I felt a bit selfish. I was glad to not be the one getting picked on.

At breakfast I sat by her and asked how she was doing.

"I just want to get out of here," she said. I wanted to leave also. We sat in silence through the meal. Later we talked and she whispered, "I'm going to run away."

My eyes got big. "Where will you go?" I asked. She told me she had a lot of family so it would not be a problem for her to find a place to stay.

Then she added, "You should come." Running away to a place where people would invite you in. Hmmmm... That seemed like a strange concept to me.

One time, back when I was living in my adoptive home, I was out playing with my friends at Turtle Park. I must have been around ten or eleven years old. When Jomaine allowed me to play with friends, she told me I had to be home before the sun started to set. This one particular day, I didn't realize it was getting dark. *Crap. I'll be grounded for a heck of a long time if I go home now.* I decided to continue to play. Once all my friends went home, I started in the direction of my home, but I turned around and ran in the opposite direction. I decided I would run away. I wandered the streets for a while, and that night, I slept under a train on the tracks. I wondered what it would be like to jump on and ride away to an unknown destination.

During the day, I collected bottles to take to the store for money and buy a bag of chips. My friend snuck me into her house one night and my other friend did the same another night. But I decided to go home even though I was scared to return because I didn't like this runaway life. I braved up and walked home. I stood at the front door and rang the bell. Jomaine opened the door and stared at me for a long time. She looked sad.

She said, "I was worried about you." She told me to come in, and we never talked about it. Needless to say, I was grounded forever. It was hard running away and I never ran away from there again.

When Christine asked me to run away, I was curious and agreed to go with her. It took a couple days of planning. We made the escape a real adventure. Our rooms had windows big enough for us to fit through, but they were on the second floor, which prevented an easy escape. We decided to tie sheets together and escape jailhouse style. In the middle of the night, we threw the sheets out the window, secured them, and climbed down. Once we were both outside we ran, giggling.

What a thrill! I'd never walked the hood in the middle of the night before. Instead of feeling fear, I felt excited. We walked a few blocks and came to this big brown house, across the street from a school.

Christine looked at me. "This is my aunt's place." She knocked on the door and proceeded to walk in. I followed her. We were greeted by smoke and cackling laughter. Nobody even realized we were there. I glanced around the living room, which was dark and felt gloomy. It was dirty and had a bad smell, like someone had burned their food while cooking.

"This is Beatrice." Christine interrupted my thoughts. I looked over at the table and there was a group of adults sitting there. The table was dirty with ashtrays heaping full, little piles of garbage all over, and a bunch of needles and spoons full of some white powder.

"Sit down." A male voice made me break my gaze. I moved clothes out of the way and sat on a ripped-up, flowery couch. I had never been in a place that looked so gross. I felt uncomfortable and feared the unknown. I tried not to make eye contact with anyone, but I couldn't help but be mesmerized by what they were doing. They filled needles up with the stuff on the spoons. Some injected themselves and others waited their turn to get their fix. They passed the needles around, cleaned them with water, and shared them.

One lady looked at me and said, "Do you know what this is?"

I shook my head no.

She said, "This will take all your worries away," and they all started laughing.

I nervously laughed. *Wouldn't that be nice.* She called me over to her. I looked at Christine and she gestured for me to join them. She fit in well. She had done this before — I could tell by how comfortable she seemed.

My heart beat hard. Although I felt fear, I didn't hesitate. Christine got off the chair and I sat down. Bella, the lady who held the needle, was older, swollen in the face, and dark-skinned, with really bad breath. She tapped the needle to remove bubbles.

"These bubbles can kill you." She winked at me and gave me a little nudge. For a moment, sanity hit me and I wondered what the hell I was doing. But before I could change my mind, my vein was filled with Talwin and Ritalin, or, as some people called it, T's and R's or poor-man's heroin. Within seconds, everything seemed foggy. My stomach turned and I tried to jump up, but everything was in slow motion.

I managed to spit out, "I'm going to throw up." Christine grabbed me and hustled me to the bathroom. I got sick for what seemed like an eternity. That was the last I saw of Christine.

Later, from where I now sat on the couch, everything grew hazy, but I actually felt like there was a weight lifted off me because I completely and utterly did not care.

"Must have been a good hit," I heard someone muffle out.

When people say some people become addicts right away, I absolutely believe them because that's what happened to me. At fourteen years old, my first drug experience was the cruelest thing that lady could have done to anyone. I wonder if she realized she had introduced me to a lifetime of addiction and addictive behaviours.

I had heard about the hood, but I had never been down there. We would drive by it when I was with Jomaine. When we would see a drunk Native person panhandling, she would tell me, "That's probably your uncle. See? That's how you're going to be when you get older."

I will never be like that stupid Indian!

I had never even drunk a beer before that night, and then my whole world shifted again. I sat there, high as hell, unable to stand up. A guy my age seemed to take a liking to me, but I was too high to pay any attention. There was a room where I was allowed to sleep. It was like an attic room. I'm not sure how I got to bed, but I woke up to this guy on top of me. I was too out of it to push him off, so I just lay there and lost my virginity. I didn't cry. I couldn't fight. I just lay there. I must have passed out because I woke up and there was another guy on me. This time, I had a bit more energy and I managed to say, "Stop," in a faint voice. I didn't feel anything, but I knew that his penetrating me meant he was sexually abusing me and I couldn't stop it.

When I woke up in the morning, I saw blood on the sheets and I was filled with humiliation and sadness. I had never even had a boyfriend before this. I felt used and abused and that night my entire world changed. I was no longer this innocent young girl. I was just another number being prepped for the streets.

∞

Within days, I was wired on drugs. I had never felt included like this before, and I liked being high. When I was high, I felt no pain, no sadness, nothing. I believe that's why I became addicted with my first shot. Christine's aunt and the others at her house treated me like a princess, except for the gross man that kept trying to grope me every chance he got. Taco was his name, and he suited it. He was short, ugly, and loud. He annoyed the crap out of me. He was always teasing me, trying to fondle me, and making inappropriate sexual moves on me. And his laugh made me cringe. I didn't understand at the time that these people befriended me because they had plans for me.

One night, the ladies were getting ready to go out, and they got me dolled up. I listened as they gently brushed my hair. They talked about getting ready for work and hoped to make some good money. I was still too shy to ask what they did.

As one of them women, Fran, put on her lipstick, she spotted me in the mirror's reflection and said, "Why don't you come? You can see what we do." She smiled.

I smiled back. "Sure."

The ladies giggled as they directed their attention to my makeup. I felt included, like people actually cared about me.

When we jumped out of the cab, there were three other ladies walking the block. As soon as they saw us, they spotted me right away.

"Who's the young beauty?" said a lady wearing the tightest short, red dress I had ever seen. She stroked my hair. I felt my cheeks get red as she stared in my eyes, and I nervously looked away. I was glad it was dark outside so nobody would notice.

Bella looked at me and started to explain what they were doing. "This is how we do it. A john will pick us up and we negotiate the price, and they always give us what we want." She threw her head back and laughed, and then continued.

"There are always sisters here watching. As soon as we jump in a car, they note the car model and licence plate and try to get the best description of the guy. That way, if we go missing they can take that info to the police."

My eyes widened and I gasped.

Fran jumped in and said, smiling, "Don't worry, that's never happened to anyone we know."

I looked at the five ladies, taking turns showing me the ropes. They were all pretty, with lots of makeup and puffed out hair held with lots of hairspray. They wore mini-skirts, dresses, or extra-tight pants — they dressed to impress.

"Go sit there." Bella pointed at a bench at the bus stop on the corner of St. John Street and Victoria Avenue. "Watch and wait. Us girls need to make some money so we can party tonight."

I looked at her nervously and quietly said, "Okay."

As I began to walk towards the step, she grabbed my shoulder and said, "Not to scare you, but I have to warn you about pimps. They'll try to take you away and force you to do unimaginable things. They'll hit you if you don't make enough money. Heck, they'll kill you if you don't make enough money in a night. And they keep your money. You'll be a sex slave. They might as well tie you to a bed because that's where you'll live until you die. Unless you somehow escape."

I looked at her in disbelief. She was scaring the crap out of me. She walked to the corner and reminded me, "Don't talk to pimps. We girls stick together."

Not much time had passed before a handsome man approached me. He was a tall, Indigenous man. When he smiled, his brown eyes glowed and his teeth shone. He had a long, slicked-back braid. I tried my hardest not to stare.

"What's your name?" he asked.

"Beatrice."

"Mine's Jack. I've never seen you here before. Are you hungry?"

My stomach growled. I wondered if he'd heard it because it was so loud. "Very. But I'm not supposed to go anywhere."

He pointed down the street, to the KFC. "We'll just go get some chicken."

"Okay." We went and I scarfed down a meal. The greasy chicken slid down my throat and the fries seriously tasted like heaven.

Jack talked about his four-year-old daughter, Kim. "My daughter's mom went to jail and I don't have anyone to care for her while I work. I know this may seem forward, but there's something about you. When I saw you, I knew you were the one I could trust to watch her. Maybe it's the innocence in your eyes, but..." He nodded as he spoke "I want you to watch her."

I looked up, my mouth filled with grease, and studied his face. Was he serious? What the heck.

"Do you want a job watching her?" He smiled coyly and sipped his cola, while he waited for my answer.

"I heard about you guys." I looked directly into his eyes. "You're a pimp. You just want me to be on the streets for you. I may be innocent but I'm not stupid!"

"No. I'll pay you with room and board, feed you, and give you drugs. You won't have to worry about a thing." Right then, a cab pulled up and inside was a lady with a little girl. Without even thinking about it, I jumped into the back seat. Jack took the front seat. The lady introduced herself and the little girl to me.

"My name is Beatrice." I smiled and looked out the window, watching the ladies on the street fade away. Although I was nervous, I was not going to show it. We drove in silence until we were just about out of town and pulled up to a motel. Jack paid for the ride and we all jumped out and went to his room. There were ladies dressed like Bella and Fran, and I remembered what they had said about pimps.

"Come with me for a sec," Jack said. I felt scared. We walked past a few rooms and I followed Jack into one of them. Jack handed me a few twenties. I stuffed them in my pocket and sat down. Jack filled up a needle and motioned for me to roll up my sleeve, explaining his expectations of me, as he shot me up with the T's and R's.

"All I want is for my daughter to be safe," he said. "You and Kim will have your own room. Once the door is shut at night, you are not to let anyone in until morning. Don't take her anywhere without my knowledge." He looked at me. "Look at me, Beatrice." I looked into his eyes. "There's something about you. I'm going to trust you. Don't let me down."

I nodded at his threat but I didn't feel threatened. I felt like he'd saved me from something that night. Those ladies back on St. John and Victoria were going to put me on the streets, and for the time being, I was being saved from that fate.

∞

I woke up and Kim was sitting on the bed, staring at me.

"Good morning," I said and smiled.

"Good morning." She smiled shyly. There was a knock at the door and I remembered that I was not to open it until morning. I saw the sun peeking through the curtain and felt it was safe to open the door. I was greeted by the smell of McDonald's breakfast as a tall, skinny, tattooed guy handed me the bag.

"Once you're done eating, Jack said to come for your morning shot."

I closed the door and put out the food for Kim and me. "Eat." I turned on the television.

"Can I eat with you?"

I patted the bed beside me. "I would love that." After eating, we washed up and I braided her long brown hair. She seemed so sweet and smart. I actually felt happy for a second, but I needed to get my shot because I was starting to feel sick from withdrawal. Jack monitored how much of the drugs I did, so I wouldn't get too wasted.

After several weeks, we moved to a hotel downtown, which was better because I could take Kim to the mall or the park. By now, Jack had complete trust in me. Sometimes, he would give me a night off and I would get to hang out with him.

I remember one night he took me to the same corner where we first met. "Notice anything different?" he asked. "Those girls are gone. I took over this corner with my girls."

Although he was one of the biggest pimps in Regina, the kind I'd been told to worry about, he never did anything to scare or hurt me as I was learning the ropes. But I was still naive.

One night, he told me to watch his "girls" because he had something he needed to do. There was a tree nearby and I climbed it and sat there, watching the women on the corner.

"Get to work!" I yelled cheekily.

Jack's girlfriend glared at me and said, "I hate you, you little bitch."

I laughed. Nobody was allowed to touch me and I knew that. So I took full advantage of it.

Jack kept to his word and looked after me because I looked after his daughter. One time, he sent me to get condoms from the store. I was walking down the street and some ladies approached me. They threatened me and pushed me around. They asked me who I was and what I was doing on *their* corner. I had to look up at the ladies because they were way taller than me and they looked mean.

"I'm just going to the store to get some condoms," I said. I was freaked out.

"Do you know whose corner this is?" one of the ladies spat out. "Mine and hers and hers!" She screamed and nodded at the other girls. She jabbed her finger against my chest. "Not yours!"

"I know," I said. "I'm just going to the store."

They looked at each other and started laughing. "Catch you on our corner again and we'll beat the living crap out of you! And you'll never forget us! Ever!" The girls pushed me out of the way and walked off, laughing.

The next day, I was walking down the street with Jack. The women looked at me alongside Jack, then ran up to me and hugged me.

"Hey what's up, Sis?"

I was intrigued by the way they changed their attitude when they saw I was with Jack. I looked at him and nodded, realizing he had earned this thing called respect. I began to change my attitude. I wanted respect too. I would sit on the street where the girls were working after dark, though I'm not sure of the exact time because our days and nights were messed up.

I loved climbing to the middle of the tree too. From there, I could see down to the end of the block. There were three women on each side of the street. It was cold and they were wearing mini-skirts and high heels. I had dressed in warm, comfy sweats and warm boots.

"Get to work. The money ain't gonna make itself," I called out to them.

"Shut the hell up, you little cheeky-assed bitch. So sick of your mouth!" They hated me because I was Jack's favourite. He let me do, and get away with, anything.

∞

A few weeks went by. All of us, including Jack's daughter, moved to a different hotel downtown. One morning, we woke up with bedbug bites all over us — gross, itchy, red bumps everywhere.

That night, I was asked to watch a room alone. I really didn't know what was expected of me, but I agreed. I sat in a small suite. It only had a bed and a few garbage bags. Bored, with no TV to watch, I wondered why this room needed protecting. *Inspector Beatrice to the rescue.* Or *nosey Nora here . . . I am!* I dug around and looked under the bed. Nothing there. I walked past a couple garbage bags and gave one a kick.

Ouch! What the heck was that? I opened the bag and pulled out a sawed-off shotgun. I felt a few more in the other bags. *Ho-ly crap!* I pretended to shoot one of the guns, now realizing why I'd been asked to guard this room.

Suddenly, there was a bang on the door. "Police! Open up!"

My heart beat so fast. I pushed the gun back in the bag, covered it with clothes, and opened the door.

"Whatcha doing in here, little girl?" one of the officers asked.

"I was sleeping. What's it to you?" I replied scornfully.

The cops came inside the room and dug around. My heart continued to beat fast. If they found those guns, I was going down. One police officer walked towards the bags. I started laughing nervously.

As he bent down, I said, "Hahaha, you want to touch my dirty undies, open away."

Stopping, the officer looked at me with disgust. "What's your name?"

After a few attempts to lie about my name, I told them my real name and was taken back to the Native girls' home.

I changed over the few months I had been gone. I was not going to let anybody bring me down. I was not gonna allow anyone to bully me or make me feel any way. I was going to stand up for myself this time and nobody was going to hurt me in that home again. And no one did.

∞

Within days, I ran away from the girls' home again, this time on my own. This time, I wasn't scared and I didn't care about my future. I realized that I could get people to do what I wanted. I had peers on the street ask me, "What do you want to do today?" As we sat around the mall's food court, I would plan what we would do.

One day, a girl named Heather, who was a year younger than me, asked me, "Can I work for you?" She was shorter than me, pretty and also Indigenous.

I knew what she meant but I was not going to be her pimp.

"I'm not sure how this will look," I said. "But we'll figure out a way to trick the johns so you don't have to have sex with them." I knew I would look after her.

The lady I was staying with was going out of town for a few weeks and asked me to house sit. I decided to work out of her home. There was a room with just a mattress on the floor. Perfect. I honestly did not want Heather to have to sleep with johns. So I told her my plan to look after her without hurting her. I'd always had a motherly instinct, even at a young age.

The first time Heather came to the house with a john, I had my friend Jax there to help me.

"Hide, and only come out when you hear me," I instructed Jax. "I just need you as backup." We hid and I heard her bring the john upstairs. My heart started racing. I tried my hardest not to overthink what could happen. If I said I was going to do something, I was going to do it. I had promised to keep her safe. I came out of my hiding spot, butcher knife in hand, trying my hardest not to drop the knife. I opened the door and looked at the john, who was in the process of unbuckling his pants.

I yelled, "What the hell are you doing with my baby sister?" I motioned for her to go downstairs. The john looked at me in disbelief.

"You're a sick fucking pig," I said. "You won't get away with this!"

"Sorry. Sorry," he said, frantically buckling his pants.

"That's not good enough. Give me all your money!"

"I don't have any."

I laughed, walked right up to him, and grabbed a wad of twenties out of his plaid shirt pocket. Maybe he was a farmer. He looked like one — all he was missing was the cowboy hat.

"Get the hell out of my house," I yelled. "You better think before doing something like this again."

He ran out of the house, mumbling something over and over. The adrenaline rush I experienced was better than drugs. I looked at Jax, who didn't even have the balls to follow me into the room, and told him, "Here's $20 for doing nothing." I scored $200. Boy, did we party that night.

I recruited another girl to work under me. She was older than me. My personality was changing daily and I never thought about the consequences. I loved being in charge. I loved the feeling of power.

This new girl brought her john to the house. Same drill. I came into the room. There stood a shorter man who was very muscular. You could tell he worked out.

"Give me your money or I'll cut you," I yelled.

He started saying, "Oh my God, no." I must have looked psycho. I honestly don't know what came over me. I had never forgotten being told that I would burn in hell when I died. I thought about this often. So although I was suicidal, I knew I would not kill myself. But I was constantly putting myself in scary and dangerous situations that had death nearby.

The john handed me $30.

I looked at him. "What the hell? You were only gonna pay my sister $30?" Sometimes when I got mad, I would see black. "This is not good enough. What else do you have?"

I followed him to his car and he gave me his weight lifting belt. He was crying like a baby. Boy, the feeling of control I had. I didn't comprehend the danger I was putting myself in. I was burning mad. But after the moment passed. I turned back to who I was. I wasn't a psycho on the daily. It was like I would change my character to reflect whatever situation I found myself in.

Once, I had an Asian john fight back. He told me, "I'm not giving you my money. Don't you know who I am?"

I walked up to him, looked him straight in the eyes, put the knife to his neck, and told him, "I killed one of you before and, trust me, I'm not scared to do it again. Now give me your money." He did and I never heard from him again.

∞

I would party every chance I got. It was a way for me not to deal with the emotional turmoil I was feeling inside. The house I lived in became popular. Every second day, we worked our hustle to trick johns and cashed in our alcohol bottles, and that would set us up for another night of partying.

One evening, I sent everyone out to get the goods for the night. At fourteen, I still couldn't pick up the booze. There was a knock at the door. I opened it and two Indigenous guys busted in. They were tall and hovered directly over me.

"So you're Beatrice. We've heard a lot about you."

"All good, I hope" Although I was scared, I put on a front that I wasn't. One of them backhanded me so hard I went flying. The other guy came in and kicked me in the ribs. I grabbed the spot where he kicked me and moaned as the pain shot through my body. I was sure he'd broken something.

One of them picked me up. "Who do you work for?"

"Myself," I groaned.

"Wrong answer." He punched me on the side of my temple and I fell to the ground.

"We aren't gonna let some young punk-ass kid mess with our bills! You think you're gonna rob our clientele and then chase them away?" He spit and yelled in my face. "You're gonna get a taste of the real world, little lady." He showed me his gun in the side of his pants. "Be back here in an hour with our money. If you don't come back, we'll find you and you'll die."

I looked into his piercing brown eyes, and something about him told me he was not lying. My hands were shaking. I knew what they were telling me to do. I'd seen all the other ladies doing it. I felt sick to my stomach at the thought. Out of everything I did in my life, I don't know why this one thing — selling sex for money for the first time — caused me so much anxiety. Maybe because that feeling of being in control of my life had suddenly been taken away.

I honestly didn't know what to do, so I nodded in obedience and proceeded to walk outside. *Holy shit— what happened?* I was no match for those two. I had no one to run to and nowhere to go. I could keep running but where would I go? I felt trapped.

∞

I will never forget the first time. I was only fourteen years old. I walked down the dimly lit street and a couple of cars passed, each slowing down. I just stopped and stood there, and immediately, a vehicle pulled up. *Ah, fresh meat,* he was probably thinking. I remember getting into his truck and looking at him with pure disgust. I knew what he was doing was wrong. All of a sudden, I was a little girl again and I began to cry.

"Is this your first time?" he asked.

"Yes," I said.

"I'll take it easy."

That made me hate him even more. When it was over, he gave me more money than usual. "Leave and don't ever come back."

I went back to the guys who put me on the street and threw the money at them.

"That's how you do it," I said. They looked at each other, grinning ear to ear. They were obviously impressed. I used that to my advantage and became an expert in manipulating people to protect myself. I learned that you do not show any emotion except anger. I learned that in order to survive out on the street, you had to be "tough" to "outsmart" the johns. I learned that it was a lonely life. I learned it wasn't a one-time thing. This wasn't as bad as I thought it would be. I hated myself anyways. And I ended up escaping from working for those guys only a few days later.

∞

Not long after, I was in the roughest bar in downtown Regina, in plain daylight, where no one questioned my age. I went to the bathroom. Sitting on the throne, I heard three ladies whispering. I strained to hear what they were saying but couldn't make out a word.

As I exited the stall, I heard, "Beatrice, Beatrice, Beatrice, who are you working for?"

I looked at those older ladies, old-timers, known by everyone in the bar.

"Sure the hell not you!" I spit out. Next thing I knew, they were punching and kicking me and pulling my hair.

"Haha. You sure?" said the scrawny woman with long hair.

"Fine. You. I work for you," I yelled. I didn't mean it. They hadn't actually hurt me. *What a bunch of wimps.* They stopped beating the crap out of me and I looked in the mirror. Not even a mark. "Wait until this fourteen-year-old gets these bitches one by one," I muttered to myself. I fixed my hair and they told me they would be watching me and waiting for me at the bar.

"Sure," I said as I walked out, not looking at them. Just as I exited the bar doors, an Asian guy pulled up in his car. I looked in the window. He was alone! As I jumped in, I looked back at the three women standing there, smiling. I closed the door and as we drove off I flashed them the finger.

"F-U," I mouthed and shook my head. I turned and looked at the Asian guy. We negotiated the price and drove off.

A few blocks down, he put a knife to my stomach and told me to take my shirt off. A man sat up from the backseat.

"Hurry, or I'll kill you," the driver threatened.

Now I was scared! We were parked behind a school. I felt a tear escape my eye. I was so mad. *What do I do?*

"Hurry!" the guy in the back seat yelled.

"Okay, okay." Shaking, I started unbuttoning my shirt.

Suddenly, he dropped the knife and said, "Don't say anything."

I looked out the window and saw a police officer walking towards the car. I heard the door unlock. I opened it and ran to the police officer, holding my shirt shut. I pointed at the guys in the car. "He had a knife on me and threatened to kill me!"

The officer pushed me behind him, pulled out his gun and yelled, "Step out of the vehicle." He called for backup and those assholes were put in that cruiser and the officer drove me to the police station. I made a statement, and they let me go. I never heard anything back from the police regarding this incident.

∞

I was sexually assaulted more times than I like to remember. *It's okay for men to treat me poorly. I'm dirty and sick and my body is for sale.*

I worked the streets for myself, most days. There was always a pimp waiting around the corner, wanting to be in charge of me, but I hated the fact that they thought I would stand on the corner for them. I was sure there was another way to survive. I hated that my body was for sale and that someone thought they could profit off *me.* I wished I could feel something other than anger. I wished I could cry. I didn't have a boyfriend yet I'd had sex. What's with that?

∞

One day while partying, I met another lady who allowed me to stay at her house for a few weeks while she went out of town. The house was a two-stories, and she gave me my own room. We partied day in and day out. I would make my money boosting: I would take peoples' orders and then steal what they wanted, and they would pay me half price. I would make a few hundred dollars a day, and that would go to booze and drugs. I realized that I could get anything I wanted or needed: drugs, alcohol, fake friends, fake laughs . . . It was all at my fingertips, but first I had to sell my body or steal whatever I could get my hands on. Sell myself and steal. Sounds about right. I ended up getting picked up by the police and brought back to the Native girls' home.

∞

I wanted to be in charge of my life and I didn't want to listen to authority because anyone who ever had authority over me always abused it. It was easier to be my own boss.

I ended up being tossed around between all the detention centres in Regina — some open custody, some closed custody. I remember one night at Paul Dojack Youth Centre. I thought I was in the warmest bed ever. I had a pillow under my head. Good enough for me. Until morning, anyways. I hated the mornings after those first nights in detention centres because I had to see the doctor. Even if I was on the run for only two weeks, when I came back, I would have to see him and each and every time this doctor would give me an internal examination. He would stick his fingers inside me and pretend to check around. I told him this is not right. Shouldn't you have a nurse in here with you, you sick pig? Twenty-three-and-a-half-hour lockup, here I come. At least he couldn't put his grubby hands in me again. I would spend a few weeks at Dojack and then go back to Dales House, a home for troubled youth, where I could run away.

Once, I ran away with another girl. We walked down the dimly lit street, raindrops glistening on the pavement. There was a light, fall breeze that touched our lips as we fake-laughed about not having a place to stay that night. I watched as two silhouettes approached us.

"Hey, girls, looking good!" We stopped as they approached us. One of the guys was extremely handsome — dark-skinned, perfect curly, shoulder-length hair, and a nice build. The other guy was nice looking but not nearly as nice looking as the other, who I found out was his brother. He was super tall with a big build.

"Where you two off to?" the handsome one asked, smiling.

My friend spoke up, as I was acting shy. "Looking for a party," she said coyly.

"Well, look no further. We know just the place. You want to join us?"

We looked at each other and shrugged. "Why not."

We followed them to their house and spent the night drinking. It became apparent that the best-looking guy was interested in my friend and not me. He was so good looking that he had the option to choose. I, on the other hand, was shy even when the drinks had kicked in. That was when I realized the brother was my only option if I wanted a bed to sleep in that night. He wasn't bad looking, but he was a huge guy, and he definitely wasn't his brother. If I'd had a home to go to I wouldn't have stayed. In my drunken state, I realized that once again my body would not be my own that night. I exploited him for a roof over my head and the alcohol that invaded my blood. And he exploited me by using my body.

Abandonment played a key role in my existence, because without a family, I had nowhere to call home. This left me with no real choice but to use my body, which gave me no satisfaction. I'd find a place to close my eyes yet again, even though after opening them, I would have to do it all again.

∞

What was this love thing? Was it the bruised thighs and black fat lips? Was it wandering down dimly lit streets after being beaten black and blue? I cried out for a mother. I cried out for a father. I cried for a big brother, or perhaps a sister, desperate for somebody to love me. Was that so much to ask for? I had no one to call my own. No place to call my home. Why did everyone leave me to fend for myself? Why did I let those who were supposed to "love me" hurt me? What was love, anyways?

Love surely was not like my mother, who'd left me as an infant with someone who obviously didn't know how to care for me. I was told that when I was seven months old I weighed only eleven pounds. I was an undernourished baby, hungry for days on end, with sunken eyes, a shallow cry, and a longing for a mommy who didn't know how to be there. Did I blame her? No, though I often blamed the system — it was the system that tore my family apart.

Abandonment caused a loss of hope in me before I could even talk. I felt confused about why I was not wanted, and that opened up a gap of loneliness that I carried through the years without recognizing it. Later, when I began my healing journey, I was able to connect the dots. I saw the damage that had been done. The loneliness had a name: abandonment. Being abandoned played a significant role in my heart's early development. My heart had felt lonely since my birth.

∞

I knew staying with the twin brothers, who I'd met while hanging out at the mall a while back, wasn't a safe place that night, but I wasn't willing to freeze to death outside. As I knocked on the door, my heart was beating hard but I didn't care. I had nowhere else to go. The door opened and one of the twins, Luke, greeted me.

"Come in. It's frickin' cold out there," he said and smiled.

I walked in and the smell of hamburger soup flooded my nose. My stomach growled. As I took my shoes off, I searched the room for the twins' dad, Dax. I could sure smell him and it made me shudder. The stench of BO and grease overwhelmed my nostrils. I spotted him serving soup to the twins, Luke and Adam, and their sister Alice. He looked at me with disgust and snarled out the words, "Grab a bowl."

I ignored his look and picked up a bowl. I walked towards the pot, and he slowly poured the liquid in as he intentionally rubbed against my breast. I bowed my head in shame and said, "Thank you." I slurped the soup standing there, trying to remember when I'd last eaten.

"You want the rest of mine?" Luke asked me.

I nodded. "Please!"

We finished eating and Dax showed me where I could sleep on the floor upstairs in an empty room. I was exhausted and wished I could have a bed — heck, even a blanket — but I wasn't going to complain. At least I was indoors.

I was startled from my sleep by a smell that exploded in my nose. I felt the hands of the 400-pound dad touch my body underneath my clothes. I tightened my eyes as if it would make it stop. I could hear him breathing in my ear. My stomach turned. I was frozen and sickened but I could not move. I just wanted it to be over so I could go back to sleep. *Am I safe nowhere?*

∞

I met a lady at the bar and she let me stay at her apartment. She shared her drugs and alcohol with me. I went to the mall and boosted clothes to share with her. After we used drugs at her house, we would go to the bar. It was crazy that the bartender allowed fifteen-year-old me in the bar. My name had started to become known, so I often drank for free. I learned how to use my innocence for profit and my street smarts got me by.

∞

A few weeks later, I got picked up by the police. The Native girls' home had given up on me and didn't want me back. I'd burnt my bridges at Dales House too. The last place to be sent in Regina is Ranch Ehrlo, a youth residential treatment facility. I was about to turn sixteen and a lot had happened in my life to change me into someone even I didn't recognize. Two years had passed since I'd first gone to the Native girls' home and I'd experienced so much pain and despair. Crazy to believe I was still alive.

Life at the Ranch was pretty chill. I was one of the more popular girls. There were three of us that kind of ran life inside the house. By this time, I didn't put up with too much crap, but bad things happened there just like anywhere else. There was sexual abuse between residents and a lot of stuff happened behind closed doors that I know the staff did not know about.

There was one staff member who was always annoying me, always in my face, trying to make me act out. One particular day, she was at it again and I decided I was gonna shake it off and go back to my room. I was on my last chance. I knew if I did something outrageous I would be sent back to Dojack, the rowdy youth centre, and I didn't want that. I ignored the petty youth worker because I knew she didn't like me. I didn't know why, nor did I care. While sitting, eating supper, she kept trying to talk to me. I asked her as politely as possible to leave me alone. I don't know what she said to trigger me. But it was dark outside, she had nitpicked at me all day, and I'd had enough. I looked her in the eyes and she stared right back at me and smirked. I think she knew she'd broken me.

I jumped up and looked at her with pure rage. "Why couldn't you just leave me the hell alone?" I screamed.

She looked fearful. As I walked towards her, she started shaking her head no. But it was too late. I grabbed her, picked her up, and threw her against the wall. She screamed for help and tried to scramble. When I got into my rages, I'd see red. I knew I was going back to juvie anyways. I let the rage take over me. I blacked out and, when I came to, I had a knife and was yelling at the ex-football player who was now a youth worker, "Back the hell up and *leave me alone!*"

"Beatrice, put the knife down and talk to me. You don't have to do this," he pleaded.

"You don't understand. She's been at me *all day*. She doesn't like me. She kept pushing me. Now I'm going back to juvie because of her! I hate her. Why did she do this?" I was so mad I finally cried.

"Okay, okay, I get it." He started to walk towards me with his hands out, trying to keep the situation in control.

Without even thinking I threw the knife at him.

When I turned around to run, I heard him whimper, "Beatrice, you stabbed me."

I turned back around and watched him fall to his knees. He was holding his heart area. I panicked and ran. Somehow, I got the other girls riled up too. "I need to get out of here," I told them. "I stabbed him!"

I ran through the field, rested behind a shed, and heard the police cars wailing by. I was stuck. I couldn't run. I had nowhere to go. I sat there and a few moments later, I saw flashlights and heard dogs barking.

I heard one of the cops call out, "Beatrice, I'm letting my dog loose, so if I were you, I would surrender."

I was tired. I didn't know the extent of the damage I'd done. I looked at my hands and saw they were bloody. I stood up and put my arms up. Within seconds, one of the cops tackled me. The police threw me to the ground and yelled, "She's contained!" After being handcuffed and thrown in the back seat of the police cruiser, I started my long night in the station. They questioned me for hours. At one point a psychologist came in and interrogated me.

"So you tried to kill him, didn't you?"

I looked at her with disbelief. "*No*, as if."

"Reading the statements, it looks to me like you were trying to kill him."

"No I wasn't. I was angry at the other lady."

"Oh, so you wanted to kill her?"

"No, I didn't. I just wanted her to leave me alone."

The psychologist left and about an hour later a police officer came in. I was so tired and disillusioned by that point that I just wanted to sleep. The officer went over my statement with me and as we were about to go to my cell, he looked deep into my eyes and said, "You're going to be charged with attempted murder." He paused and then asked, "Why did you want to kill him?"

I sat with my head down and couldn't think straight anymore. *Did I try to kill him?* I began to wonder. But deep in my heart I knew I hadn't. I quietly mumbled, "I didn't want to kill him. I'm so sorry." Tears ran down my face. I was done.

I received two ten-month sentences for the charges of assault with a weapon and assault causing bodily harm, to be served concurrently. I spent much of my sentence in twenty-three-and-a-half-hour lock-up. I looked forward to the half hour shackled walk around the track, as I was constantly rebelling towards the authority. I was not yet sixteen years old.

I started to gain the trust of one of the guards, whose name was Sheena. We would talk and I started to open up a bit about my past. I told her what my adoptive brother, Frank, had done to me as a young girl and how I believed that was the root of a lot of my anger. She listened and I respected that.

One day, I was sitting talking with her and she suggested that I call Jomaine and tell her what had happened. I didn't want to because I didn't think she would believe me. But a couple of days later, after thinking about it, I decided to call.

"Hello," Jomaine answered in her nice phone voice.

"Hello, its Beatrice. I need to talk to you about something."

"What is it?" she asked. After a long pause, I told her what Frank had done to me as a child. Without hesitation, Jomaine denied that he would ever do that. "He would never," she said, gasping.

"But he did, Mom." That was my last attempt at ever confiding in her.

"No I don't belie—"

I didn't let her finish the sentence. I looked at the guard. I was so mad I slammed the phone down, over and over until I broke it.

"Beatrice, Beatrice, stop," the guard screamed. "Talk to me."

I jumped up and pointed at her. "*You.* I trusted you!" I grabbed her and started wrapping the cord around her neck. She fell to the ground. I stopped. I walked to my room and locked myself in. *I will never trust anyone again.*

I finished doing a ten-month stay in Dojack Youth Centre, a closed-custody juvie. I was a ward of the government and had outstayed my welcome at every open-custody group home.

When I turned sixteen, the worker assigned to me said, "You're an adult now. You'll have your own room at the YWCA. We'll give you food vouchers every month as long as you live there. Stay out of trouble." She laughed.

The smell of that worker's perfume made me sick, and as I grabbed the food voucher from her grimy hands, I swore at her. I walked out and slammed the door, almost breaking it off its hinges. I didn't care. I had nothing except the bag of clothes I'd accumulated while I rotted in Dojack.

∞

I made my way to the room at the YWCA. It was small, with just a bed and a dresser. I would have to share a bathroom with a bunch of old women. I was not impressed. I threw my clothes on the hard single bed and did what I knew best. I walked to the mall to find trouble. And that's where I met my son's father.

At the Cornwall Shopping Mall, I hung out with a girl named Sheila, who I had recently met. We'd hit it off right away. While we waited for her boyfriend, we sat and chatted up a storm until two guys walked towards us.

"Hey, baby." The tall skinny guy grabbed my friend and kissed her. "How ya doing?"

She giggled, looked at me, and introduced me to his friend. "Hurbert, this is Beatrice. She's my new bestie."

He smiled at me and I smiled back. Something about him made my heart sing. Was it his long brown hair or his genuinely handsome smile? Whatever it was, when he asked if I wanted to hang with them for the day, I agreed. Why not? It was something to do. We walked over to his apartment, Sheila and I footsteps behind.

"What do you think of him?" she asked. "He's totally into you."

"Yeah." I smiled. "He's alright."

In the alley, we started talking. He made me laugh. Nobody really made me laugh. We joked around, all of us with no care in the world.

"This is where I live." He pointed to a rooming house.

"Looks like a dump," I joked.

He walked up to me and pushed me. I stepped back and fell over a two-foot fence, banging my head on the ground. Bam! I saw lights and heard laughing. I opened my eyes and looked at the three of them chuckling. All I could do was laugh with them. I felt embarrassed and my head hurt, but I didn't want to look like a baby.

I ended up staying the night with him and when I woke up, he was gone. I looked on the bed, and my white pants had blood on them. Shoot, I got my period and I needed to go back to the YWCA to change. I wrapped my jacket around myself and walked the ten blocks.

Hurbert and I pretty much shacked up right away because I was lonely and he didn't expect me to go out and make him money. I didn't realize that he had two kids already, but in just a matter of months, my life changed forever.

I missed my period for three months. I went to see the doctor and sure enough I was pregnant. *I'm pregnant. I'm pregnant. Oh my gosh, I'm pregnant.* The next thing that came to my mind was, *what is Jomaine going to think?* I instantly felt shame.

I didn't tell many people that I was pregnant. Throughout my pregnancy, I still wore my jeans. I spent many of my days at the mall, boosting for money, and I would steal my clothes and whatever else I needed.

∞

My baby daddy was abusive throughout my pregnancy. Once, when I was in my last month of pregnancy, he came back from a night of drinking and he was angry. Good thing I lived across the street from the hospital because in the process of giving me a beating, he kicked me in the stomach. All I remember is feeling like my baby did a complete flip. I went to the hospital because that scared me. They checked me and did an ultrasound. Everything looked okay. The doctor kept asking me if I was okay, and asking me questions like, who did this to me, and would my baby and I be safe in my last month of pregnancy.

I nodded my head up and down. "We'll be fine," I said with my head down. I knew that I couldn't go back to Hurbert's because he would know I went to the hospital and I was fearful for my baby. My friend, Sheila, came to see me at the hospital and I told her I couldn't go home. She asked her sister, Darlene, if I could stay with her.

Darlene allowed me to stay with her because she knew I was homeless and I was days away from giving birth to my son. I had just turned seventeen, and I didn't have a clue what to expect. I was in the kitchen making pizza pops in the microwave. As soon as I pressed start, I started to feel a sensation like I was peeing myself. It came in trickles and I felt a tad cheap, even though no one was at the house to witness it. Feeling embarrassed, I went to the washroom, sat down and continued to pee, or so I thought. But it wouldn't stop. I managed to get to the phone, but I didn't know who to call other than Jomaine.

When she answered the phone, I told her that I could not stop peeing. She frantically told me that my water broke and the baby was on his way. She told me to call an ambulance, which scared me half to death and said she would meet at the hospital. I hung up the phone and went and sat on the toilet, crying because I was panicking. Luckily, Darlene walked into the house at that point. She calmed me down and was surprised that I didn't know anything about the beginning of labour. When Darlene drove me to the hospital, she gave me a bunch of towels to sit on and I had a garbage bag wrapped around me so I wouldn't get the seat of her car wet.

Someone let my baby's dad know I was in labour. Always drinking, this guy. When he walked in the room, he reeked of alcohol and smoke. He smiled real hard as he staggered over to the bed.

"Baby's coming, hey?" He laughed.

Darlene looked at him and told him, "Shut your ugly face up."

"Fuck you. Why are you even here?" he squawked.

Sheila piped up, "She left after you gave her a licking. She was homeless, you idiot."

Their voices started to get louder and the nurse came in. I was crying. When she arrived, Jomaine tried to comfort me. She and Darlene went at it because Darlene couldn't understand why Jomaine was trying to play mommy now, when she hadn't been there when I was alone on the streets and pregnant.

"Enough!" the nurse yelled. "My goodness! This poor girl is in labour."

Everyone started arguing again. They were loud and stressed me out. It was like I couldn't hear them anymore. I saw their mouths moving, the anger in their eyes, and their arms flailing in all directions. I closed my eyes. I wanted them all to go away and just leave me alone. The pain was so unbearable. I felt like I was dying.

"Beatrice," the nurse said, snapping me out of my state. "Who do you want to stay in the room with you?"

I needed a mommy, now more than ever. I looked and pointed to Jomaine. That pissed everyone else off. But I think I chose her because, in a weird way, I still wanted to believe that she loved me and wanted to support me.

The nurse checked me and told me I was fully dilated and needed to go to the delivery room.

∞

The delivery room was so white and clean and bright. They put my legs up in position to push and I felt enormous pressure. I swore and then apologized to Jomaine.

"It's okay." She smiled.

I told the nurse, "The baby is coming."

She said, "Not yet!"

"Yet," I yelled. I looked up to the corner of the wall close to the ceiling, at a mirror focused right on my . . . oh my gosh! I saw my son's hair. "Move that mirror!" I yelled to the nurse.

I didn't want to push anymore. His head seemed huge. But all it took was one more push and Terence was out. A 5 pound, 5 ounce little baby boy. After they weighed and washed him, they handed him to me. I blankly stared at him. I did not have a clue what to do. All I knew was I was a mom now. But what did that even mean?

Later, the nurse wanted to show me how to breastfeed. I thought breastfeeding was the best option, so I sat in a circle with other moms as they breastfed. The nurse said she would be right back and I held my baby.

"You know when I breastfeed I get a sexual feeling," one woman said.

"Who the hell would say something like that!" I looked at her with pure disgust. "What's wrong with you?"

When the nurse came back, I pointed at the lady and told the nurse, "That woman is a weirdo." I got up to walk back to my room. I was so angry I was in tears. So when the nurse tried showing me how to breastfeed, I couldn't do it. I couldn't believe that woman had ruined this bondable experience for me, a moment between a mom and her baby.

When I look back on this time, I believe my reaction was because of the sexual abuse and how my body had been used for sexual purposes. I did not breastfeed any of my kids because I could never get what that woman said out of my head.

I spent ten days in the hospital. I didn't have a home to go to. I didn't have a clue what to do. The hospital's social worker decided to get me a hotel room for a few days while I figured out where I was going to live. I was also given food vouchers. Thankfully, they gave me a few outfits and diapers and formula to last my baby for a little while.

Terence and I made a great pair. I was catching on to this mommy thing. If Terence cried, it was because he was hungry, needed his diaper changed, or just wanted to cuddle. I could take care of that.

I made the mistake of telling Hurbert where I was staying and he came to see me. I needed to have a shower, so I asked him if he could watch Terence, and he agreed.

I hopped in the shower and the warm pressure of the water felt so good on my tense muscles. Eyes closed. Peacefulness. Then I heard the door creep open. Seconds later, he was in the shower with me, forcing himself in me. I begged him to stop but he covered my mouth and continued penetrating. I felt my stitches rip. The pain hurt so bad. When he finished, he got out of the shower. I cried uncontrollably and lay in a fetal position. The water had turned cold. I lay in the bloody water. *Why me? Why do I always have to get hurt? When will everything be okay?*

Thinking back on the day Terence was born, this naive girl hadn't even realized her water had broken. How the heck was I to know what to do with him? I had no choice but to figure it out on my own. I never did go back to Darlene's house. I wonder how long it was until she found the pizza pop in the microwave oven.

∞

I loved my small baby boy so much. He smelled like love. The love Terence gave me was unconditional. This was love and made me want another baby. He brought me so much joy that on the hard days I just held him and loved him. Not being nurtured with love or being taught how to parent when I was growing up, I had to learn the hard way how to raise my son.

I did not know that Social Services could help with housing and food, so I was homeless and penniless with Terence. He and I spent many hours hanging out in the mall where I stole for all his needs. One cold day in the dead of winter, I bundled him up and we walked to find food before we used up his last bottle. I carried him in my jacket. I was a pro at stealing — that's how we ate. I was cautious as I entered Safeway. In the baby aisle, I captured all his needs — I stole diapers, premade formula, and two extra bottles. I looked both ways and, on my way out, grabbed a premade sandwich. My stomach growled in anticipation of the finest bite.

As I walked out the doors, I felt a tap on my shoulder and a man said, "Ma'am, come with me please. You have something that doesn't belong to you."

Shame overtook my body. I put my head down. Did he not understand my son would soon be hungry and this was the only way I could feed him?

The police came and picked me up. One of the officers asked me, "Where will you go?"

"I have nowhere to go."

"We can't leave you on the streets. You don't have family?" the blonde officer asked me.

"I have my adoptive mother, but I'm sure she won't take me in."

"We have to try," she said. So they drove me to Jomaine's house. The officer let me out of the back seat with Terence in my arms. We walked up to the door and the officer rang the doorbell. I stood there feeling anxious, as Jomaine opened the door.

"Beatrice was picked up for shoplifting," the officer said. "We need to drop her off somewhere. We can't leave her and her baby on the streets. Can they stay the night?"

Jomaine shook her head no. The officer looked at her in disbelief. With no look of sympathy, Jomaine just said no and shut the door.

The officer looked at me. "Sorry." She hugged me as we walked back to the car.

I shrugged my shoulders. I knew it would happen.

I had to go back home to Hurbert. He would laugh and mock me and hit me whenever he pleased. He'd call me a slut and a whore and remind me how everyone hated me and that nobody wanted me because I had a child. Not only that, but now I had another one on the way. I hated that man more than ever, but I had nowhere else to go. Big and pregnant with another baby boy, I was devastated and fell into a deep depression.

∞

I would run away when I couldn't take the abuse, but I would always end up right back with him when he came back apologizing. He broke my spirit. I felt like nothing, I hated myself, and I cried much of each day.

One time, I was staying at my friend Sheila's, and her daughter, who was a couple of months older than Terence, was walking around him. At seven months, my son still did not want to roll or crawl. I ended up taking him to the specialist at the hospital, where he spent ten days being picked and poked at. I found out he had minor cerebral palsy and he had a stroke in my womb. I knew that must have happened when Hurbert had kicked me in the stomach.

∞

I was so depressed and couldn't get out of bed, so Hurbert invited his mom to stay with us for a few days. She hated me and was not afraid to show it. My hair was down to my butt and she talked me into getting a perm.

"Sure," I said. What a mistake. After she fried my hair by keeping the chemicals in too long, she cut it above my shoulders, turning it into a frizzy mess. I looked at my reflection in the mirror and cried. I looked at her.

"Looks good," she said, kind of snickering, She always took little jabs at me.

Hurbert walked in and started laughing. "What the hell happened?" They both giggled.

∞

As I lay in bed, Hurbert came in. "Mom made bullet soup."

I got up to eat because I didn't want to argue. There was a bowl sitting on the table for me. Hamburger and potato rolled in flour, dumped into boiling water and then thickened. I ate it even though I wasn't hungry and then went to lay back down.

A couple of hours later, I woke up when my stomach cramped. I ran to the bathroom and my bullet soup exploded into the toilet. The cramps were unbearable. I kept throwing up all over the porcelain throne. I managed to wash up and crawl back to bed, sweating profusely. I started to convulse in agony and kept dry heaving. I was worried about the baby inside me and knew I had to get to the hospital. Hurbert watched Terence.

The doctor determined I had severe food poisoning. I spent a week in the hospital, unable to eat or drink anything. Even the IV liquids didn't want to stay in my body. The woman in the hospital beside me felt sorry for me. This was the worst sickness of my life. Funny thing is, nobody else who had eaten the soup got sick. That is when I became a germaphobe.

∞

This one time, while I was still pregnant with my second son, I was sitting at the table while Hurbert, his brother, Doug, and his wife all drank. I was forced to sit there and watch, stone cold sober. I had to listen to Hurbert cut me up and laugh at the way he mocked me and called me names in front of everyone. I would put my head down in shame and just wish to be in my bedroom alone.

"Quit being a party pooper." Hurbert slapped me across the face.

"Don't let him treat you like that," Doug said. I looked at him, stunned that he would say that, because there were many times I saw his pretty wife black and blue after a night of his drinking.

"Really?" I asked.

"Yeah, stand up for yourself," he said.

Well that was all I needed: permission. I looked at Hurbert without an ounce of fear.

"I'm sick and tired of your bullshit." I stood up, clenched my fist, and punched him with all my might! I knocked him right off his chair. I jumped on him and punched him over and over again, just like boxers do when they know they're going to win the fight. That's when Doug pulled me off him. He laughed as he looked at Hurbert, whose nose and lip were a bloody mess.

"You better watch it, Hurbert. You pissed this girl off," Doug taunted.

I walked to the room where Terence was sleeping. My heart was racing. *What the hell did I do?* I was scared and excited at the same time. I locked the door and sat on the bed, shaking. I held my belly and sobbed quietly. I wasn't sure I would be brave enough to face Hurbert alone the next day. I knew everyone had left because the loud rock and roll music stopped playing and the drunk laughter had stopped. I lay on the bed and cried myself to sleep.

After a while, I woke up to the sounds of Terence playing in the crib. I forced my eyes open, swollen from crying. I looked at him and he smiled. I began to cry again, unsure of what to do. I didn't leave — I wasn't sure where I would go.

∞

A few months later, I had my second son. This time, I delivered my baby alone in the hospital. It was lonely and scary, but I didn't need or want the drama that I'd experienced with my first delivery. I held him so close and he smelled like heaven. I named him Nathan. My boys were eleven months apart and the doctors wanted to tie my tubes. They'd suggested it after the birth of my first son, and I considered it again now. *But what if I want to have more children some day?* I declined.

∞

Hurbert, the kids, and I were on the move again. We moved into a small, two-bedroom house in the east end of Regina. The older couple who had lived in the house moved to a nursing home, so their children rented it to us. The home was old fashioned, the furniture and walls decorated like it was the 70's. But it was workable for my little family.

We had two babies now, and Hurbert was already drinking away our welfare cheque. He sent me to the grocery store to get our month's supply of food. I was so excited. At seventeen years old, grocery shopping would be a first for me — a real adult thing to do alone. I hopped the bus and headed to Safeway, smiling and looking out the window. Walking through the store, cart in tow, the smell of fresh bread tickling my nose. As I paid for our food, I wondered how I would carry the six bags on the bus, but I did it. They were heavy and the two-block walk to our home from the bus stop just about did my arms in.

I walked in the door, smiling about my accomplishment.

Hurbert glared at me. "Holy shit! How much did you spend?" He jumped up and dug through the bags, looking for the bill. He grabbed it and looked at me with disgust. "A hundred and fifty dollars. What the hell were you thinking?"

My heart pounded as he charged at me and started strangling me. I began to lose my breath and woke up on the floor, unsure of what had just happened.

Hurbert was glaring at me. "Good, you're awake. I thought I killed you."

I felt the back of my head and there was a big goose egg. I must have hit my head on the door when I fell. I looked over at the groceries, still packed.

"Get the hell back on that bus and return those fucking groceries."

I started to cry. I couldn't bear the humiliation. "Please, no."

He got up and kicked me in the head. "Now."

I will never forget how stupid I felt when I returned everything and how the cashier looked at me. I don't know if it was with pity or disgust. All I know is I walked out of there with my head down in shame. I would never again go over budget or want to shop by myself.

∞

I ended up staying with a friend that night, and within a month, Terence, Nathan and I had our own place. It was short lived. We lived in a cycle of abuse, leaving, apologies and returning to Hurburt. Although I had no plans for the future, I knew I wanted to be the best mom I could be, even if that meant I had to teach myself the basics. *Love your children with all you can and never lay a hand on them. Feed them and clothe them and tell them you love them always and forever. Never make them feel unwanted because that's the ugliest feeling ever.*

I had a dream that I was in a house in the city. I was young, maybe three years old. I could smell fresh bannock. It must have just come out of the oven. We were in the downstairs apartment of a house, and there was a woman. I didn't see her face, but I felt her love. I knew it had to be Mama. I was on her lap, and she was holding me tight. She nestled her cheek to mine and squeezed me tight. She kissed me on my forehead.

"Eat, my girl," she said. I watched her smother the jam on the bannock. I giggled in delight. When I looked at her, love filled me. I grabbed the jam-filled bannock and bit it.

"I love you, Mama. I love you so," I said, and then I woke up.

∞

Hurbert wasn't a big guy, but somewhere along my road in life, I'd learned it was okay for men to hit me. Trust me, he was not a man. The abuse kept getting worse. I have scars all over my face from being punched in the face during that time. I stayed because I believed Hurbert's lie that nobody would want me because I had two kids. I felt alone and stranded but enough was enough. Although I didn't care about my own well-being, when the abuse turned on Terence, who was only three at the time, I knew I had to leave again.

I walked to my cousin Lisa's house, and Hurbert caught up with me and told me to get the hell home. I kept walking, holding my son as Nathan walked beside me. Hurbert punched me in the mouth. He split my lip, and my bottom tooth went right through my skin. Terence started screaming. I looked at him and he was covered in blood. I started screaming, feeling his face, praying it was my blood.

My other cousins Roy and Ryan came running out of the house and chased Hurbert so they could beat him up.

Then Lisa grabbed my son and checked him over. She looked at me with tears in her eyes. "You have to leave him," she said.

Nathan held onto my leg and cried. I held his head to my leg and I looked at Lisa, realizing she must be seeing blood everywhere. I was in so much pain I could barely speak. I muffled out the words, "Where will I go?"

"You can stay here."

I put my head down in shame. "Okay."

A week later, I saw Hurbert at the store and he apologized over and over again, "Please give me another chance. I promise I have changed."

I believed Hurbert's lie that everything would be different, that he would change, and I went back to him.

∞

It was not until a whole year later that I decided to leave for good. The abuse had gotten so bad. Over the course of a few months, I had packed little plastic bags of clothes and hid them around the house.

One night, Hurburt came home drunk, which was strange because he would usually stay out all night, cheating on me with different women. This night I knew I was leaving. I had rustled up enough courage. This was it. I fed Hurbert supper and patiently waited for him to pass out.

My heart beat so fast I could practically taste my fear. I heard Hurbert snore. It was time to go. I had the stroller ready just outside the bathroom window. I gathered all the bags that I'd stashed around the house and threw them outside. I picked up both my boys and said, "Shhh" as I tiptoed to the door. When I opened the door, it squeaked. I shuddered. "Please don't wake up, please!" I whispered.

He didn't. I opened the door fully, ran to the stroller, put my boys in, hooked the grocery bags on the stroller, and ran as fast as the stroller would go. I didn't know where

I was going, but I knew we would never go back. I turned to look behind me and tried to catch my breath. I must have run six blocks, and thankfully I had no followers.

I stopped and looked up at the sky. The sun was no longer in sight. It would be dark soon. Where was I going to go? I couldn't go to my cousins' because they were mad at me for always going back to Hurbert. I saw the Lawson indoor swimming pool. I pulled on the door and thankfully it was open.

We entered and I stood there, looking at my sons. Their big eyes greeted mine. I felt my cheeks warm with my tears. I wiped them quickly and smiled. I didn't want to upset them. I walked to the phone booth and sat down on the bench. I didn't have a quarter to make a call, nor did I have anyone to call. I grabbed the phone book, opened it, and wondered where my next stop would be. I flipped through the pages, starting from the beginning. My eyes were drawn to some bold numbers for a transitional shelter. I paused. *What's a transitional shelter? Would they help us? How would I call to find out?*

I looked up as an older gentleman walked by. I asked, "Do you happen to have a quarter on you?" He looked at me with disgust and kept on walking. I put my head down and shook it. What was I going to do?

A woman walked by.

"Do you please have a quarter?" I pleaded. "It's an emergency." I'm not sure if it was the black eye I was sporting or the desperation in my voice, but she dug in her purse and handed me her change.

"Thank you so much."

She smiled and walked away. I picked up the phone and dialed the number in bold.

There was an answer. "How may I help you?"

"I . . . I . . . I . . . need help," I forced out of my mouth.

"What kind of help?"

"I'm eighteen, I have two sons, and I have nowhere to go. Their father is always beating me up, and I'm scared that one of these days something's going to happen to me. I have no one to turn to, nowhere to go. I'm at the Lawson pool and I had to bum a quarter to make this call. Please, can you help me?"

The lady on the other end said, "We'll send a cab for you. Wait by the front doors if it's safe."

"Okay." I hung up the phone and hugged my boys. Fresh tears rolled down my cheeks. I felt a rush of relief. There actually was a place to go, a place where my boys and I would be safe, at least for the night.

We sat there waiting patiently for the cab to arrive. My heart was beating like crazy because I didn't know what to expect, but I knew that whatever it was couldn't be as bad as what we were leaving. The cab picked us up and I put the stroller in the trunk. We drove for a while and then pulled up to what looked like a mansion to me. I had never been in a house of that magnitude before. I grabbed my boys and our few belongings and walked up the stairs that led to the home that offered me a hope of rescue. I rang the doorbell and an older White woman appeared at the door.

"Hello," she said politely. "Come in. You're safe now."

I smiled nervously.

"Please, have a seat." I sat down in the chair as she asked me some basic questions. "Who are you? What's your age? What are your boys' ages?" Then she asked me, "What brought you here tonight?"

Tears escaped from my eyes like a flood. I couldn't hold them in anymore. I felt safe enough to voice my thoughts and concerns.

"I'm tired of being hit and put down by the guy who says he loves me. Every time he goes out and gets drunk, I'm scared how he's gonna act when he walks through the door. I'm tired of being cheated on and made to feel like I'm worthless and have nothing to offer this world. I'm tired of my sons seeing me cry. The abuse is getting worse. He hits me when I'm holding them. I just need out."

She was writing, but then looked up at me. "You're safe now. Let's talk some more tomorrow." She guided us to our room, up two flights of stairs.

"Goodnight," she said as she closed the door behind her.

There was a double bed, a crib, and a dresser. The room looked comfortable and inviting but there were way too many pillows. *Who needs that many pillows? I guess they're for decoration.* They did look pretty.

That night, as I lay in bed feeling restless, I couldn't move because one boy was in each of my arms, hugging me tightly. Tears rolled down my cheeks because I felt so lost, yet safe. So scared, yet excited for change. All these images of abuse danced in my mind as I drifted off to sleep. Nightmares disturbed my sleep as they always did. I woke up. My sons were playing quietly on the bed. They were such good boys. Not a care in the world.

"Hi, Mommy," they squealed as my eyes greeted their cheerful smiles. I thought they must be hungry. So we went downstairs.

Two other women with their children sat at the table, already eating. One of the ladies had a face full of bruises and she looked incredibly sad.

Days turned into a week, and the workers tried to help me set up a plan to stay safe and away from my abuser. They helped me find a house and furnish it. But I always had a hard time staying alone. Hurbert would always sniff me out and come lying his way back home. "It will never happen again," and "I love you, please take me back," he would beg and I always did. It was a sick cycle because the abuse didn't end; it always got worse.

During this period, I would run away from him and I moved around between shelters. There were three in Regina that I frequently visited. I was beginning to trust the workers, especially at the YWCA. A worker there named Carol always treated me with respect and tried to show me my worth and dignity, an idea that was foreign to me. I loved the fact that my children could play and laugh without someone telling them to be quiet. There was no yelling at the shelter and no hatefulness. But it was not family, and that's what I missed. I couldn't run to a family member's house — a safe place — so when I ran, I ran to the shelters.

Unfortunately, I would get lonesome, for what, I don't know, and I would go back and forth between the abuse and shelters, over and over again. Until one day, I realized the only way I could keep myself from going back to him was if I left the city. So that's what I did.

∞

I had been looking for my brother, Vince, for years and heard he was in Edmonton. That's where I decided to move. The shelter in Regina transferred me to a shelter in Edmonton and Social Services paid my way.

Once we arrived, the shelter workers were helpful and assisted me in finding my brother. I discovered he was in jail, about to be released within a few days of our arrival. He was able to call me on the phone, and I was so excited to hear from him. I had not seen Vince since my fifth birthday party thirteen years prior. His voice over the phone was deep. I wondered how he looked. We set up a time to meet as soon as he got out of jail. I had so many questions that I couldn't wait to have answered.

Two days later, I bundled up my boys and we were off to meet their uncle. The workers told me how to get to the LRT train station and my heart beat frantically with excitement. I opened the shelter doors. Outside smelled like stink. It was a cloudy, fall afternoon, but that didn't stop me from smiling. I pushed Terence in the stroller since it was hard for him to walk because of his cerebral palsy, and Nathan skipped beside me.

"Momma, where are we going?" Nathan asked.

I looked down at my two-year-old boy and said, "We're going on an adventure."

He squealed with delight. I walked a few steps on the cracked sidewalk. I looked to my right and there was a black cat, dead, with its head cut off. I gasped in horror as I covered my sons' eyes so they wouldn't witness something so grotesque.

I hurried along the busy street and there were so many cars and people walking with green jerseys. There was a football game right beside the LRT station. I could see the stadium two blocks away and knew I was going in the right direction. I walked against the traffic of green jerseys and Nathan skipped along beside me.

Then someone yelled out of his truck, "You're going the wrong way, you stupid Indian."

I turned my head to see if they were actually talking to me. He gave me the middle finger. What the heck! That was out of nowhere. I walked faster to the station. I hoped this was not how my day was going to continue. I shook it off and smiled at the nice day.

I reached the spot where I was supposed to meet Vince. I began to shake. How would I recognize him? I barely remembered what he looked like as a child. Just then, I saw a tall Indigenous man with thick, curly, long hair and dark tinted glasses, who was walking towards me.

"Vince?" I said, looking puzzled.

"Yes, sister." He smiled as we awkwardly hugged. I was happy but I had never experienced healthy hugging from a brother and was a little taken back.

"Are these my nephews?" He kneeled down.

"Yes." I smiled as I introduced my boys to their uncle.

Vince was staying at his friend's place in a high-rise downtown, and he took me there. He said there was an empty suite beside their place. I signed papers and moved in with Terence and Nathan a few weeks later. The shelter helped me furnish the place.

I would like to say that life was all cheery from then on, but that was far from the truth. I took a lot of acid, drank to bring myself down, and smoked pot. One time, I was so high on acid that I thought the soccer field lights were the yellow brick road from the Wizard of Oz. I skipped out onto the balcony. My brother grabbed me and shook me.

"You're getting out of hand."

I laughed with no care in the world. The next day I woke up and my mind was numb because I had been drinking and doing drugs daily. I wanted to stop but I didn't know how.

After a few months in Edmonton with my boys, I didn't know how I was managing. I was sitting at my four-seater kitchen table, my mind loopy. I couldn't remember the events of the night before. I slurred my words. My sons danced to *Sesame Street* and giggled as they mimicked the television. I felt lost. My head pounded to the beat of *Elmo's World*. I covered my ears in desperation, to make it stop.

I knew I couldn't go on like this, but being in a new, big city, I didn't know which way to turn. This was many years before the Internet, so I picked up the phonebook and desperately searched for help. I came across an organization called Boyle Street Co-op and called them.

I spit out the words. "Hello, I need help."

The person on the other end of the line was very helpful.

"What do you need help with?" she asked politely.

I didn't want to reveal too much, so I asked what they offered. I could hear what sounded like a brochure being opened and this was confirmed when she started reading. I heard her say the word "school."

"Yes! Stop! What do you offer for schooling?" I'd finished Grade 8 when I was court-ordered to stay in school, which felt like a lifetime ago. I managed to pass with a D because my teacher said she could not imagine spending another year with me. They said they'd pass me as long as I never came back to the school, which included not attending graduation. The only time I'd ever touched the floor of a high school was when I'd gone for a tour, so I was intrigued.

We set up an appointment for someone to come see me at my apartment to discuss the schooling opportunity. I hung up the phone, pleased with myself. I had a week to pull myself together.

I kept my cute little one-bedroom high-rise apartment clean. It was furnished, and my sons and I had moved in with only a couple of suitcases and a bag of toys. So when I forgot about my appointment, and the buzzer rang, I wasn't too worried about the appearance of my apartment. I was worried about my lack of sleep, though, and how Beatrice was going to present herself.

I buzzed the woman in and paced back and forth nervously. I ran over to Terence and tucked his striped shirt into his blue jean shorts. I checked the boys' diapers and made sure there were no surprises as I heard a knock. Nathan squealed in excitement and ran to open the door. I hurried over and unlocked the deadbolt, which was out of his reach, and I let him open the door.

"Hi!" Nathan yelled out and smiled from ear to ear.

"Hi," the lady said and she squeezed his cheek.

I guided her to the table and we both sat down. She glanced around my apartment, trying to be as inconspicuous as possible.

"I don't know how you keep it so clean in here with two little boys," she said to break the ice. I laughed a nervous laugh and tried my hardest not to fidget. She explained the program to me and said I was a good fit. I didn't feel any judgment from her. She was there to help. I decided to attend school and hopefully get my life back on track.

I was ready to start at the community school, where I would begin Grade 9, and set out to find daycare for my sons. Within a week, I had my boys registered at the YWCA's daycare and I hopped the train to school. After a month of going to school, I realized I was four months pregnant. I couldn't make sense of some of the decisions I was making but I still tried to attend school and keep my kids in daycare.

It took me a few months to recuperate from all the drug use. I moved away from the high-rise into a two-bedroom apartment in a rougher part of the neighbourhood. It was closer to the train station and honestly, I just needed a change. Unfortunately, I fit in well because I was rough around the edges. I continued school and kept in touch with the woman from Boyle Street Co-op. I had someone to talk to, even if it was mostly surface talk.

I was having a hard time sleeping. My belly was huge. It felt like I was carrying a ten-pound baby. While I tried to sleep, she was wide awake, kicking me right in my ribs. I looked at the clock and saw it was just after 2 a.m. My apartment was finally quiet.

Since arriving in Edmonton, I had met a lot of people. While I couldn't sleep, I thought about how I was being used. I needed to sleep and not think. I had school in the morning.

Even while I was in school, I still managed to take Terence to his physical therapy once a week. He was given a walker to help him get around faster and he loved it. He loved chasing his brother.

I was struggling to manage my two boys and my pregnant self but that didn't stop me from taking them to the park daily and chasing them around the monkey bars. They'd giggle with delight as I called out, "Mama's gonna get you."

Running with his walker, Terence wasn't as fast as me or his brother, so I would slowly chase him and he would throw his head back, mouth open wide, and say, "Momma, you can't get me."

I'd catch them, wrap them in my arms, and smother them with kisses. "I love you so much." The stress of everything felt like it was killing me, but every day I made sure I spent valuable time with my children, and it was these times when all the troubles of my world faded away.

After restless nights of tossing and turning, waking up at 7 a.m. didn't come easy, but I received money from Social Services and part of the agreement was that I stay in school. I didn't mind because it kept me busy and out of trouble. I looked over and my boys were sound asleep. I had better get up. At three and four years old, getting the boys ready in the morning was no easy task. But first, I had to go see who was out there in the rest of the house.

Opening the bedroom door, I heard snoring in the living room. The floor was covered with sleeping bodies. I counted six plus the bro on the couch. I knew everyone — there were about eight of us who hung out. My boys called them uncles and aunties. Even though I was only related to two of them, my brother and my cousin Shelly, we were all family. When I needed help, they were there, as I was there for them, whether it was just sitting and talking about our broken hearts or going to the bar and chilling up an ex. My boys always had food, toys, and sometimes way too much candy. Every once in a while, we would lose a bro to jail but we always looked out for each other. That was the main thing.

There was never a fight in my place, nor arguing, unless it was between a couple, and that would end real quick. My boys were never in danger. It was the total opposite. One day, we came home from school and one of the uncles gave my sons five bucks each to go to the store. Well, the next one called them over and gave them ten dollars each, and that carried on with all six bros. My boys' hands were full of dollar bills. Terence knew to stuff them in his pocket, but Nathan, at the age of three, was not sure what to do. I ended up taking them to the mall because they had $100 each. Plus, the bros gave me money too. My boys and I never went without. I always had money in my pocket and we were dressed to the nines.

My daughter, Shanice, was born, and she was healthy and absolutely beautiful. She and my boys were my world. And although I honestly didn't know how to love myself, I sure knew how to love them. Did I love them the "conventional way" or the "right way"? I don't know. I stole food to put on the table. I stole their clothes to jazz them up. Taking off drinking and drugging were not good parenting skills, for sure. But that's all I knew back then. I wished I'd been taught different, or wanted to be different, or better, in society's eyes. At nineteen years old, with three children, I had no clue what I was doing.

I got back into alcohol heavily and began losing control of myself again. I left my kids at friends' places for days on end until they got ahold of me and told me they were going to call Social Services. But I just couldn't get control over my life.

∞

I remember one time Hurbert found me in Edmonton. I allowed him to see his boys. He was going to take Nathan out to eat, so I gave him $20. I bathed Nathan and got him ready, and he was so excited. When I went to bring him out to Hurbert, I discovered he was gone. I could feel Nathan's disappointment as he shook and cried in my arms.

I had already notified the brothers and they found him at a skid row bar. They waited for me there. I walked in with eight big, built men. I looked at Hurbert and the girl he was sitting with as they drank a pitcher of beer.

"You're drinking your son's food money," I said in disgust. He turned to say something and I walked up to him and slapped him. I looked at the girl and told her to leave. Hurbert sat there, fear in his eyes. I was thriving off his fear. This must have been how he'd felt all those times he'd beat me black and blue.

The brothers looked at me. "Want us to finish it?"

"Yes," I said and walked away. I never asked what happened, but since then, whenever I saw Hurbert, he would run the other way. And that was okay with me.

∞

Social Services allowed me to take time off school for maternity leave. At this time I had a new boyfriend, Logan, who was a good looking, green-eyed Indian, fresh out of jail — just how I liked them. A few months later, Logan got stupid and went back to jail. Every evening he was allowed to make one call, and every night I waited for his call. As soon as I hung up, I was out the door, leaving my brother to babysit.

Sometimes I would be gone for days. Eventually, Vince would track me down and threaten to call Social Services. I'd come home with money and drugs and give them to him, and he would leave happy. It worked every time. I was getting tired of the cycle though. I needed a longer break and I couldn't think of anyone but Jomaine to watch my kids for a few weeks. I wondered if she would.

Before I could second guess myself, I picked up the phone and dialed Jomaine's number. When I heard her voice, my heart jumped out of my chest. I was so nervous to ask her to watch my children. She wouldn't understand that I needed a break, so I lied and told her I was going to go to treatment. I wasn't intending to go to treatment, nor did I think I had a problem. But I needed a break and I had no one else to turn to.

"Mom," I said, "I need help."

"What is it now, Beatrice?" Her tone was condescending, as if I was always asking her for stuff, even though I hadn't seen her for years.

I spat out the words. "Can you please watch my children while I go to treatment?"

There was the longest pause ever. "Let me think about it. Call me back tomorrow."

The next day, I called her back and she said yes but with conditions, which she stated firmly. She would take my two younger ones, but I would have to find other arrangements for my oldest because she said all three children would be too much for her. She would watch them for twenty-two days and that was it. And I'd better be going to treatment.

Vince agreed to watch Terence. My cousin, Shelly, and I drove from Edmonton to Regina the next day after stealing a car and gas. I dropped my two children off at Jomaine's and then we headed back to Edmonton right away.

Outside Regina, we were in a high-speed chase, caught by the police, and put in police cells in the town of Broadview. When we were let out of jail we hitchhiked home.

Back in Edmonton, I spent the days hanging with Terence and the nights partying. It was a never-ending cycle. A few days after I had dropped my other two children off in Regina, my phone rang.

"Beatrice? Is that you?"

I was silent. It was Jomaine and I'd told her I would be in treatment. Fear washed over me.

"Yes, I am going to treatment today," I lied.

"Yeah, right." She hung up the phone and I just sat there blankly with my heart beating a mile a minute. What would she do? I was still scared of her. I knew she couldn't physically hurt me, but I was terrified nonetheless.

The next day, there was a knock at my door. I was served with papers saying that Nathan and Shanice had been taken by Social Services. I was shocked! How could Jomaine call the welfare system on me? I had to go to the Social Services building and figure out what my next steps would be.

I put Terence in the stroller and we headed downtown. At the worker's office, I was greeted by a man who walked us to a room and straight out asked me what happened. I explained to him that I was tired and needed a break for a couple of weeks. I said I had to lie to Jomaine because she would never have taken Nathan and Shanice if I hadn't said I was going to treatment. I explained that I didn't have family and she was the only family I'd ever really known, other than my brother, an auntie and some cousins, but they couldn't take the kids. I just needed a break. I was planning to pick them up in a couple of weeks.

The next day, the worker came and checked my apartment. I was moving again. He told me that as soon as I moved he would bring my children back to me, but I had to have food in the fridge and my home had to be safe. After getting settled, I was reunited with my children.

∞

Logan was released from prison again, but shortly after his release I called the police on my green-eyed boyfriend because he was crazy and abusive and beat the crap out of me. Someone called Social Services — I'm not sure who — and I was told to go to a shelter or lose my kids if I went back to him.

When I found out I was pregnant again, I was scared; Logan had just been put in jail because of me. What was I going to do? I was not ready for another baby. I was having a hard enough time raising these three.

I made one of the worst decisions of my life, something that haunts me to this day. I had an abortion. *If I have an abortion, then I will never go back to him.* I knew I couldn't look him in the eye, and as unreasonable as that sounds, I went through with it. And I didn't see Logan ever again.

The scars on my outer body are *not even close* to the scars inside me. Sometimes to this day, I still cry about that decision. It still hurts so bad that I took a blessing and discarded it.

∞

I stopped drinking so much; it was easier for me this time because I was not drugging. I was a weekend drinker, but I wanted to quit for good. I wanted to be the best momma I could be. I may not have been taught the skills, but I knew that as I child, I had craved hearing "I love you," hugs, fun times, and laughter. I didn't hit my kids, nor would I ever. I wanted them to know that I would do everything in my power to make them happy with what little we had.

I was so excited for Terence's first Christmas concert at school. Nathan sat beside me and Shanice sat on my lap. We made sure to sit right up front. The principal announced the schedule and Terence's class would be first. As the principal walked off the stage, the kindergarten class walked on. As soon as I saw Terence's smile, a tear escaped my eye. I was so proud of him.

"Momma, look — brother!" Shanice screamed in delight.

I looked at Nathan and his eyes glowed with delight. Terence was in the front row and his eyes scanned the crowd. Nathan started waving hard and as soon as Terence saw him, he smiled and started waving.

"Momma, look at me."

The crowd awed, and I couldn't stop crying. I was so happy in that moment.

∞

I decided to go back to school. I wanted to be a good parent. I didn't drink for six months and I was proud of myself.

Terence had to go to the hospital to get eye surgery for his lazy eye. I was kissing him up and so were his brother and sister, reassuring him that we would see him soon. We went to the waiting room and the social worker that had been on my case came to see me. Although he knew Terence had his eye surgery that day, I was still surprised to see him.

"Beatrice, do you mind if the nurse takes the kids for a bit? I want to talk to you about something."

"Sure," I told him. I smiled and kissed my boy and girl and watched them as they skipped off with the nurse. "What's up?"

"We're taking your kids away." The worker pulled out a pink piece of paper.

"What? Why?" What did I do? I couldn't think of anything. I was doing everything that was asked of me and more. I was trying my hardest to be the best mom ever. Six months — that's a lifetime to be clean.

"The lady downstairs from you said she saw you piled up, fighting on your front lawn, and called, concerned for your children."

"No, *no* she's lying. She's just mad because the kids run around upstairs and she's always banging her broom on the ceiling, telling me to shut them the hell up. I promise, please don't take my kids. *Please.* Piss test me. Do whatever you want. I'm clean, I promise."

"Sorry, Beatrice, we're taking the kids and that's final. There's the court date. He pointed to the paper he handed me. "See you then." He got up and walked away. I sat there in disbelief, tears running down my face. How would I carry on?

I was in shock. I didn't understand what had just happened. I went to my supports at Boyle Street Co-op and cried my eyes out. I cried and cried and cried. I was so angry.

"It's not fair! I tried so hard to do everything they asked me to."

I walked five blocks to skid row and spent the next couple of weeks back to the same old shit. Snapping out of it two days before court, I got my kids back but I didn't want to stay at that house. I moved in with my friend Kara. Unfortunately, I'd gotten a taste of the streets while my kids were gone and I was having a hard time coming back from it. In the back of my head, I knew I was not good enough in the worker's eyes, or in the eyes of society as a whole, but I tried. I just didn't try hard enough.

∞

Now I can look back and see my dysfunction, but when you're in the midst of it, you're blinded by the instinct to survive. While I was staying at Kara's house, we got into a fight and she kicked me out.

"Where will I go?" I looked at her in complete fear.

"I honestly don't care, Beatrice. You need to get your act together. You need to dummy the hell up!"

Normally I wouldn't allow anyone to talk to me like that, but I let it slide. I started to panic. I looked at my three children. They were so innocent. I was so angry, I wanted to cry; if only I could.

"Get your jacket and shoes on, boys." I dressed Shanice. "We need to find somewhere to stay before it gets dark."

I loaded Terence and Shanice into the stroller, and Nathan walked with me as we went off to who knows where. This was one of the times I realized what a mess I was. I had this agonizing ache in my heart. I could barely swallow. I felt so alone. I was homeless with my three children.

Nathan skipped ahead, no care in the world. Shanice babbled and turned her head to look at me. "Momma, love." Her eyes glistened.

I turned away for a split second because she broke my heart. Stopping the stroller, I grabbed all my kids and held them. I didn't want to ever let them go.

"I love you all so much," I whispered. "I love you so much."

After walking for what seemed like forever, we hopped on the LRT. I hoped I wouldn't get asked for my ticket. I had no money to pay, and they would kick us off at the next stop if they caught us. We got off at the stadium station and walked to my friend Sharlyn's house, downtown. I banged on her beat-up door and waited for her to answer.

"Hey, can we stay here for the night? We have nowhere to go."

"Sure, Sis, come in."

Sharlyn opened the door wider and we walked in. She was a short, hard woman who I'd met downtown. She was mean but not to me. Her house was a mess. Beer bottles and needles lay everywhere. I felt sick that this was where I'd brought my kids, but I didn't have anywhere else to go. She led me to the room we could stay in.

"Thanks, Sis, I'll get you back," I managed to say without breaking down. The door closed and I looked around the room to make sure there was nothing dangerous that my kids could get into.

"Go lay down, sweeties. Mommy's gonna go clean up the ugly stuff out there." I changed my mind and lay down with them until they fell asleep. My heart was breaking in two. I couldn't keep them here. It was too dangerous. I got them up.

"I'll see you later," I told my friend. "I can't keep my kids here. Thanks so much, though."

"I absolutely understand, Sis. I wouldn't want kids here either."

Walking to mobile services, a place to go after hours instead of Social Services, I only hoped they would help me. I don't know who I prayed to, but I prayed that we would have a good night's sleep together. But that would not be the case. My world was about to shatter and I couldn't stop it.

"What's your name?" the worker asked me.

"Beatrice."

"What do you need?"

"I need a place to stay for the night with my children. We have nowhere to go."

"You don't have family or friends to go to?"

"Obviously not, otherwise I wouldn't be here, would I?" I said out of desperation.

"Well, there's nothing we can do for you. Sorry."

I looked at her in disbelief. *"What?"* You're going to turn me and my children away in the dark of night? I thought you were here to help. I only need a bed for the night. I will see my social worker in the morning and figure everything out. I always figure it out. I *always* do."

"Sorry, Beatrice. Looking at your record here, it states that you've lived in fifteen places in two years. Who moves that much? And why? You're putting your children in bad situations and I cannot allow this to happen any longer. We're going to keep your children and put them in a safe home until you can get it together. You will not be leaving with your children. We can do it the easy way or the hard way. It's up to you."

I sat there with Shanice sleeping in my arms. I looked over at my boys, both asleep in the stroller. How had I gotten to this point in my life? Why the hell was my life so fuckin' hard? And why had I been allowed to bring children into this world if I was only going to break their hearts? I squeezed Shanice so hard and tears streamed down my face. I knew what I had to do, but it was going to be so hard. I could no longer put them into the bad predicaments that I was always putting myself into. It wasn't fair to them. They deserved more. Even if I couldn't save myself from the choices I was making, I wanted to protect my kids from them. They deserved a family that cared for them. Obviously, I couldn't do it.

I felt like my heart was going to cave in. My world was shattering. I wanted to scream and yell, "Why, God, *why?*" The police were at the desk, talking to the worker, and one looked at me. Looking up at her, I truly thought she saw the brokenness in my eyes. She turned away real quick, bowed her head, and walked out of sight.

I sat on the floor, holding my children close. I wished I had kept my damn mouth shut earlier that day and not argued with my roommate. I was nothing but a fuckup, but I knew what I had to do. I had to think of them and not myself. Tonight, I had to provide them with a safe roof over their heads and food in their bellies. And that was something I couldn't do.

"Beatrice, sign these papers. They say you're allowing us to take your kids for the night because you couldn't provide shelter for them."

The words on the page were all mumbo jumbo to me but I signed the papers. I looked at the worker and asked, "Will I be able to see them tomorrow?"

She handed me a card. "Call in the morning. It's late, Beatrice. We have a placement for them. We need to take them now," she said, with a stone-cold face.

"Okay." Tears filled my eyes as I walked toward the exit. I wiped them real fast so I could take a good look at my babies. They sat there, looking at me. They probably didn't have a clue what was going on, because I didn't.

"I love you so much," I whispered. "I love you so much."

For the rest of the night, I sat on a bench, staring at the building where I had just left my children. The police were called to come and remove me in the early hours of the morning.

"Just leave me the fuck alone! Leave me alone!"

"Walk or you're going to jail!" they threatened.

I didn't care anymore what happened to me. I hated myself so much I wanted to die.

That night, I slit my wrists. Despite fearing death all my life, now I didn't care if I went to hell. I sat there in a pool of blood, hoping to die. All I remember is my friend, Georgette, walking through the backdoor of the place where I was staying. She saw me sitting on a chair in the middle of the kitchen floor, falling into unconsciousness.

"Beatrice! What the hell did you do?" she yelled.

My eyes started to roll back and I felt a sting on my face where she'd slapped me.

"Wake up!" she screamed.

"Leave me be," I mumbled. "I don't want to live."

I hated myself but it obviously was not my time to die because I made it through the night. I ended up healing on my own and have the scars to prove it.

∞

Though I lived, I hated every day of my life. There was no way to get my kids back in my current condition and I knew it. I was a major fuckup and my children deserved someone who could raise them and meet their needs. I couldn't provide that for them, no matter how hard I tried.

I called Muskowekan Reserve and told them to come get my kids because I didn't want them to be raised in a White home. I hated White people — they thought they were better than me. They'd done the same thing to my mom. White people had taken us away from her, and look how I turned out. I wanted to give my children a chance at life — a chance I never had. I hoped someday they would understand that I didn't give them up. The system did everything in its power to make sure I didn't succeed. Well, they had won. I hung up the phone and then punched the wall until my knuckles bled. Then I made my way downtown. There was no way I could stay sober any more. No way.

No matter how hard I fought for the kids, I was never good enough in the worker's eyes. I sadly gave up the fight. I lived on Edmonton skid row and drank and did drugs and was back in survival mode. I turned to partying, drinking, drugs, and working the streets when I needed, just to forget — to numb the incredible pain in my life and especially the loss of my children. Losing them broke me beyond comprehension.

The day I gave it all up, I walked straight down to the roughest bar on skid row in Edmonton. I hated myself more than ever. I wanted to die. I hated my life. I hated everyone and everything that wasn't my children. I'd lost my children. I'd lost the only reason I had to live. I didn't know how to live without them. I'd lost myself. Days turned into weeks and weeks turned into months, and I wouldn't die.

I put myself in dangerous situations. I scrapped in bars. I had a knife pulled on me. It got to the point where I was kicked out of every bar on skid row because of fighting or ranking out. One time, I was so angry I grabbed a chair and threw it through the window. That was the last straw. The staff knew me by name, and they told me to leave and never come back. I didn't care. Whenever I went to bed, I would make sure that I had drugs or alcohol beside me; if I didn't, when I woke up I would be too sick to move.

∞

One day, a friend's boyfriend told me that there was a woman walking around asking someone to kill me. She was willing to pay $300. He laughed because he said he wouldn't do it for any less than $500. He was joking, but he said, "You better lie low for a while because someone could easily take her up on her offer."

That's when I decided to head to East Vancouver with another friend, her boyfriend, and my new boyfriend Joe. Joe was an alcoholic, which was better than a drug addict because we didn't have to scam for so much money. I stopped using hard drugs for a while but continued drinking every day and night. We got on social assistance as soon as we hit East Van and got a place in a rundown hotel. It was so bad that when you turned off the lights you could hear the cockroaches and rats running around the room. When you turned the lights on, you could watch them scatter. It was a small room with dirty walls and the smell in the hallway was disgusting.

One night, we were partying in the bar downstairs. My boyfriend was on edge, and he was unpredictable at times. That particular night was no exception.

"Are you okay?" I asked.

"Yeah, yeah, don't worry about it," he scorned. I continued to drink with my friend and then she disappeared for a while, so I sat with the guys and listened to their bullshit. When the bar was closing, my boyfriend and I headed upstairs. On the way, we passed a Black man.

My boyfriend looked at me and asked, "Who's that?"

"How am I to know?" I said. "I was with you all night."

We proceeded to our room and once the door closed, he punched me right in the eye. "I asked you who that was!" he yelled.

I was baffled because I didn't have a clue. I felt panicky inside and all I could do was mouth, "Seriously."

He continued to punch me and I fell to the ground. That's when I felt a kick to the face. I must have passed out because when I woke up I was lying in a pool of blood. I felt my nose. It was burning and one of my nostrils was ripped right off my face. In the mirror, I looked hideous. I was crying because I didn't know what the hell had happened.

I was so sick of the abuse. I decided I was going to stay disfigured, so no man would ever look at me again. I went to bed and passed out. When I woke up a couple of hours later, my face throbbed. Screw it. I had to go to the hospital. When I walked in, the nurse gasped and took me into a room right away.

"What happened?"

"I'm mixed up with the wrong crowd." I lowered my head.

The doctor came in and examined my nose. "It might be too late to stitch this up. When did it happen?"

"Last night, probably five hours ago."

"I'll do my best, but it's already starting to heal this way." The doctor froze my nose and stitched it up — seventeen stitches inside and seventeen outside.

"You're one lucky girl. If you'd come in an hour later, there would have been nothing I could do." Looking at me with great compassion, he said, "You better find yourself some new friends."

"Yes, thank you." I looked at him. *If only.*

I thought about where I would go. I knew I couldn't go back to Joe. This was the worst incident and I was not about to lose my nose to this asshole. I found out where the homeless shelter was and I stayed there for a couple of days until the swelling went down. The doctor had done an amazing job stitching it up. You wouldn't know what had happened unless I showed you.

I hit the bars again. One time, I didn't make it back to the shelter in time and had to sleep in the park with all the other homeless people. I got up and went to the bar, got a hit, and worked the street. That was my cycle. I barely stood on the corner. I did most of my business in the bars.

∞

"What's your name?" he asked me. Jaxson was a large Indigenous man and handsome. I wondered why he felt like he had to pay for a night out.

"Beatrice." I smiled coyly at him, playing hard to get. We went to his apartment, where he passed out. I dug around and stole $100 extra.

The next day, I was sitting in the bar when he walked in. He saw me and walked over to me. He looked pissed.

"Why did you steal my money?" he demanded.

I just looked at him and shook my head. "I don't know what you're talking about." I didn't feel intimidated by him because I was in a bar full of people. He stared at me for a long time and then walked out. I stayed in the bar for a bit, not wanting to face the long walk home, but that night, it was dead and I was tired. As soon as I walked outside I saw him standing there.

"Hey." He smiled at me. "Don't worry about it. I must have put it somewhere else."

"Oh, yeah, probably." I felt relieved that he wanted to drop it.

"You want to come over?" He pulled out a couple of bills.

"Sure." I should have trusted my gut and not gone with him. As soon as I walked into his apartment, *bam*, I received a whack to the head. I flew to the ground and tried to jump up, but all I saw were stars. *Bam, bam!* Right to the face.

"You *stupid bitch!*," was all I heard before I was knocked out. When I came to, he was lying on my arms and punching me over and over again in the face. I blacked out again. When I came to again, he was raping me.

He strangled me. "Say the Lord's prayer!"

I couldn't open my eyes. They were swollen shut and suddenly my life flashed before my eyes. You know how they say that, in that moment before you die, things move in slow motion? They did. I saw myself as a child and I saw my children. I saw all my life's regrets. I gagged. I knew I was dying and I couldn't fight back. I had nothing left in me.

After I woke up, I tried my hardest to open my eyes. I saw a silhouette of him lying beside me. I wondered what time it was. I wondered why I was alive. I couldn't tell if he was sleeping or awake. My heart beat fast. I lay there, helpless and hopeless, scared that if I moved, he was going to finish me off. I could feel him breathing on me.

"You awake, sweetie?" he asked.

"Yes," I said.

"Are you hungry?" He sounded playful.

"Yes," I said.

"Okay, I'm gonna go downstairs and get us something to eat, okay?"

"Thank you," I said, as politely as I could.

"You'll be here when I come back, right?"

"Of course." I gasped as my heart started beating hard. He walked out the door and I sat up. *Is he trying to trick me? Is he waiting on the other side of the door? Do I take a chance?* I didn't pause to think any longer. I grabbed my clothes and opened the door slowly. I didn't even second guess myself. I ran down the hall. I ran down the stairs. I started to feel safer. I bashed the doors open.

I squinted and saw that the police station was right there across the street — thank God! I ran across the street, busted into the front doors and fell to the ground. I was safe. I was naked, but I was safe. I must have passed out because I woke up in an ambulance with an IV attached. I listened to the medics speaking softly.

"She's lucky to be alive."

In the hospital I found out that I was pregnant with my fourth child but the doctor told me I was having a miscarriage. I felt so bad. When I looked in the mirror, I didn't recognize myself. My whole face was swollen and I looked like a chipmunk. I had a major concussion and bleeding on my brain so I had to stay a couple of days in the hospital.

It was a miracle that I came out of there alive. The biggest miracle came when I was getting ready to have a D&C, a procedure to have my baby removed because the doctors had told me I lost my baby girl.

"I'm sorry," the technologist said. "I have to check for a heartbeat. It's just procedure."

I cried because my heart was broken.

"Listen," she said.

When I listened, I heard a faint heartbeat. My baby was alive.

∞

I couldn't stay in Vancouver. Even though Jaxson, the man who had assaulted and almost killed me, was in jail, I feared for my life.

I returned to Regina where I gave birth to a beautiful baby girl, Desirae. In the hospital, tears rolled down my face as I held her, looking at her peaceful, sleeping body. I held her close to my troubled heart because I couldn't stop thinking of my other children. I missed them terribly and I so much wanted them to meet their baby sister. How could I parent Des with so much guilt in my heart? I looked at her and knew that I would not allow her to feel my sadness. I would parent her to the best of my ability. I would love her and cherish every moment we had together. I kissed her on the forehead. "I'm so thankful for you," I whispered. "You saved my life."

∞

Although I had quit using drugs while I was pregnant, I picked it back up right after her birth. My new boyfriend and Desirae's step-dad, Freddie, was in jail during much of the time we were together. When he was out, he was abusive — not as much physically, because I would fight back, but mentally and emotionally. He beat me with his words and he would cheat on me. Sometimes, I thought it would have been better if he'd hit me rather than cheat on me.

When I got pregnant with my fifth child, I went to treatment right away. At twenty-three weeks my water broke, and at the hospital they said there was nothing they could do. The baby was too small to deliver and I would just have to see the pregnancy through and pray that the baby survived. I went home and hugged my little girl, Desirae.

Within a week, I could feel that it was just my baby in my belly. There was no amniotic fluid left. I carried my baby for a few more weeks and then went into labour. Because it was a dry birth it was the worst labour I'd ever experienced. My baby boy Elijah James was born at 1 pound, 3 ounces. He had the faintest cry ever. The nurses whisked him off. The doctor came in and told me Elijah's lungs were not developed and if he survived, he would have medical issues all his life. He said my baby was on life support, but I should take him off. I wished that I had someone to call because I didn't know what to do.

"I have nobody, doctor. What should I do?"

"Take him off," the doctor said and walked away.

WOLF WOMAN • 117

I sat there crying, alone. I tried calling the jail, where Freddie was once again, and told the staff my situation. I told them I needed to talk to Elijah's father, but they never let me. Sitting looking at my tiny baby, I couldn't hold it together. I didn't want to be selfish, but I wanted him to live.

The nurse came into my room the next day. "So what have you decided?"

"I want to do the least selfish thing." I walked into the neonatal intensive care unit and sat by his incubator. The nurse opened it up and put Elijah in my hands. He was so small — so beautiful and small—he fit into one hand. I kissed him and held him, my pain unbearable, tears falling. They took him off life support and I heard a little gasp. My heart . . . my heart. I sat there for who knows how long, in shock. The nurse told me she needed to take him. I sat there, brokenhearted.

I tried to call his father again to tell him what happened, but I never heard anything back. I had met a friend, Max, in treatment and I called him because I didn't know what I was supposed to do next. I didn't know anything about planning a funeral. His mom answered the phone and she told me I could bury him on their reserve and she would help me with everything I needed. I didn't know what else to do or what other options I had, but at the time, I was so filled with grief that I agreed. I lived close to a community centre. I talked to a pastor there and he agreed to lead the service.

When Freddie got out of jail, he was expecting to see a baby, but there wasn't one. One Sunday afternoon, we went to go visit our son's grave. Elijah's uncle came with us to bless his journey the traditional way. It was a somber walk up the hill to where Elijah had been laid. Standing there, his uncle said a prayer in his Native language, which I didn't understand, and he smudged Elijah's gravesite with sweetgrass. He explained in English that it had come to him, when he was praying, that every time we see a hawk, we should know that Elijah is watching over us and he wants us to know he loves us. I closed my eyes. Tears streamed down my face as I wished desperately that he was here in real life.

When I opened my eyes and looked at the grave one more time, I saw a baby feather. "Look."

I picked it up and showed his uncle and he said, "That is a baby hawk feather. Elijah wanted you to know that he is here with you two and loves you always. He is reminding us to remember him every time we see a hawk."

My heart exploded with so much grief. I picked up the baby feather and kissed it.

"I love you, Elijah. I love you so much," I whispered through my tears.

We tried straightening out our lives by moving to Fort Qu'appelle, Saskatchewan.

∞

Des and I were listening to Buffy Saint-Marie's, "Darling Don't Cry." Desirae was three years old and, with a sheet wrapped around my shoulders, I would pretend to fancy dance as she giggled. Desirae followed behind with a beach towel draped over her shoulders. This brought back memories of the powwow I'd attended as a teen in Regina. The drum beat was the same rhythm as the beat of my heart. It felt like a connection made in heaven.

My favourite part of that powwow had been the women's fancy dance. The dancers looked like colourful butterflies floating across the arena, hitting every note on key with grace and ease. As I watched them, I felt like crying, wishing that I'd learned to dance or even understood the significance of it. I watched as parents dressed their children in their regalia, adjusting every piece with love and joy. What a beautiful sight.

∞

The months passed. I went to school, got my GED, and began visiting my older children. Things were starting to look up. A few months into the visits, the social worker took me out for coffee. He stared at his coffee cup for a long time and then finally looked up.

"Beatrice, these visits are hard on the kids."

"What do you mean?" I asked.

"It's disrupting their routine. Two days before the visits, they get excited and don't listen to their foster parents. Then you visit and for two days afterward, they are sad. And when they finally start feeling better, it starts all over again. It's not fair to the kids, these visits."

I stared at him blankly. "Well, let me raise them, then. They're my children."

"Beatrice, you know we can't do that. They're wards of the government. Once they're old enough, they can decide if they want to see you or not. But until then, do the right thing and step back from their lives." He got up and walked away.

I sat alone in a little hometown café called Grandma's Cafe, staring blankly into my coffee cup. Head down, I couldn't move. I couldn't cry. I didn't want to feel.

Why?

∞

I would not visit them again while living at the Fort. I had always wanted only what was best for my children. I did not want to hurt or confuse them anymore so I chose to listen to the worker. Elijah's dad and I stayed sober and we both went to school. We were a cheeky, loud couple, and many times drew too much attention to ourselves. We stayed with his mom, Elizabeth. I wasn't always sure she was too fond of me. One day, Des was really sick and Elizabeth asked if she could make her some tea.

"Sure," I responded, knowing it would be a traditional tea. At this time, I wanted so badly to learn who I was as an Indigenous woman. I knew that his mom was well respected in our Indigenous community, and I was eager to learn from her. Des tried to drink the tea, but she didn't because she didn't like the smell. Elizabeth asked me to hang a bundle of tea leaves on a tree in the backyard.

A couple of days later, I started feeling different. I heard voices and saw black images, and when lying in bed, I would hear footsteps walking around me. I asked Freddie if he was experiencing any of this but he said no.

Then, when we were playing cards, I looked up at him and said, "I feel like I want to kill you." I smiled at him.

He looked at me with fear, like it wasn't funny despite my smile. He and his mom went for a drive.

The next day, they took me to a medicine man who performed a ceremony on me. As part of the ceremony, he sucked on the skin on my shoulders and little sticks that looked like porcupine quills came out of me. After the ceremony, we never talked about it again, and I went back to being my old self. This experience opened my eyes to a spiritual realm that I never understood before. I have always wondered how this related to me hanging the tea leaves in the tree, but I didn't want to think too much about it.

∞

I continued my rocky relationship with Freddie, which became worse than before. I got pregnant with my daughter, Kasheena and moved back to Regina with Desirae. After my daughter Kasheena was born, the three of us moved back to Edmonton. Although I tried to stay sober, I was a mess.

The first time I met Heath, he was super nice. I thought he was handsome. His tight curly black hair made him look exactly like Shaggy, the singer. But he being nice changed real fast. Within weeks, I discovered that Heath had a temper. People respected him wherever we went because he was tough. We hung out in the roughest bars in Edmonton. Getting into fights with other people, we really made a name for ourselves.

Heath's mother had a place just outside of Lac La Biche, three hours from Edmonton. He asked if I wanted to bring my girls and stay out there with him for a while so we could both sober up again. We were at the point where we were using drugs and drinking daily, and I was leaving my girls with a friend who saw more of them than I did. We had known each other for less than a month, but it felt like this move would be good for both me and my girls. I agreed that a change of scenery was a good idea.

The three-hour drive to his mom's place went fast. Five Mile Corner was a Métis settlement, ten minutes from town. There was no running water. The house was heated by a woodstove. It was a smaller house that looked like someone was trying to maintain. The grass definitely needed to be cut, but the land was beautiful. There were birch trees in every direction and it was as though the sky was brighter and bluer there. The lot and surrounding area looked inviting and the view was breathtaking.

When we got out of the car, the air was crisp and clean and the girls ran out giggling, holding hands, and skipping.

"Welcome to my home," Heath said and smiled. I felt a peace in my heart. I felt okay with my decision until I saw the outhouse.

I looked at Heath and asked, "Is *that* where we use the washroom?"

"Yes, but only during the day." He laughed. "At night you can use the slop bucket."

"Oh. . ." I felt gross inside. I'd never used an outhouse before. This would be interesting. The girls continued to run around as Heath and I entered the house.

"Come on, girls. Get in here. Don't want you to get eaten by a bear." Heath laughed.

"Are you serious?" I asked.

"Well, no, but there's always a possibility."

Entering the house, I saw that it was homey. There were knickknacks everywhere and there was a picture or ornament on every piece of brown wooden wall. The house looked well-lived in. An older lady came walking out of a room, rubbing her eyes. She spotted her son and her eyes brightened.

"Heath, my boy, you're home!" She walked over and hugged him tightly.

"Yes, Mom."

She was a short, thin lady with grey, curly hair and big, old-time glasses. Now, this house suited her.

"This is Beatrice and her girls," he said, introducing us.

"Welcome," she said. "So glad to have my boy home."

After our long drive, Heath and I decided to take a quick nap. We put a movie on for the girls and lay down in Heath's small room, which contained a single bed and a dresser. The room was cozy and kind of felt like camp. I drifted off to sleep right away.

"Mom, Mom," Desirae whispered. She was four years old now. "The movie's over."

I slowly opened my eyes, grabbed Desirae and hugged her. I realized Heath was no longer beside me, but at some point Kasheena had made her way into our bed and was starting to stir from her own nap. As she started to wake up, I wondered what Heath was doing but did not feel comfortable enough to come out of the room. The girls and I hung out in the bedroom. I heard clunking in the kitchen. A beautiful aroma seeped through the crack of the door, making my belly growl. Des and Kash played quietly on the bed as I lay patiently waiting for Heath to come get us.

Finally, the door opened. "Come out," Heath said.

I jumped up, excited for supper.

∞

Days turned into weeks, and living in the country was exceptional. The winter was worse because we woke up frozen, but it was definitely a homey home. I enjoyed the country air. I enjoyed the sobriety of life. Heath's family was so nice, but Heath had a temper. He didn't direct it at me, but he was starting to get restless and irritable.

One night, when his mom stayed in town, Heath didn't come home from his cousin's. He drank and left me and the girls home alone while it stormed. The storm was so scary; the power went out and my girls and I huddled on the bed. Although I was scared, I acted brave for my girls. The storm lasted most of the night and I finally dozed off in the wee hours of the morning.

The next day, when Heath came home, he apologized. I quickly forgave him, asking him not to leave us like that again.

That night, I told Heath that I was pregnant, and he was so excited. *Maybe this time everything will work out and I'll actually be happy.* But that feeling was definitely short-lived.

The first time Heath hit me, it was a boxer's punch to the head. I got two black eyes and a cut-up mouth, accompanied by an "I'm sorry, it will never happen again." It left me feeling desperate, alone, and terrified because I was in the middle of nowhere. Even though his mom was in the house, I felt alone because she would intentionally stay out of the way. When Heath was sober, he was the nicest, most thoughtful, caring individual. But when he was drunk or high, he was the scariest person I'd ever met. Even the police were afraid of him.

I finally gave birth to Dalreesha, and everyone loved her, especially Heath's mother. But I could not let Dal cry or his mother would give me heck. When I cleaned, I swept with one arm and held Dalreesha in the other. I loved my girls so much, and when we were home alone we had so much fun. But when others were home, there was tension. The abuse got worse and worse. While I was home, everyone always ignored the abuse, but when we went to town and I had a black eye, his sisters would give him hell. Not that it changed anything. It sometimes made things worse and got him madder at me when we got back home.

∞

One day, I bought a disposable camera. I wanted to take pictures of my girls. This was before the Internet and smart phones. I was super excited to get the pictures right. I dressed my three girls in similar clothes and covered the old, beat-up couch with a floral sheet as a backdrop.

Dal started crying. She did not want to smile. She would rather be snuggled in my arms. She was cute as a button. Her pale skin, red nose, and curly black hair inspired me to give her the nickname Snow White. Her sisters sat still and grinned, showing their teeth. Dal wailed at the top of her lungs.

"Dal, just one picture, please," I pleaded with her.

She fought the camera. I was losing hope that I would get a good picture. Still, I snapped away. Today, as I look back at those pictures, I love the realness and innocence they showed. They are my favourite pictures of Dalreesha. Des and Kash are smiling hard and Dal is trying. The picture shows her pale face and red button nose. The girls all looked so beautiful and it made me feel happy to take their first photos.

∞

The final straw with Heath came because he kept drinking. Even if I didn't want to drink, I would, because I knew he was going to become abusive. There were times when I would be in bed, sleeping, and he would drag me out by my hair, in a terrifying drunken state. One night, I knocked back beers as fast as he did, trying to keep up. His cousin was drinking with us as we all played cards. Heath started arguing with his cousin, but everyone was terrified of Heath because he was tough and mean. Suddenly, he looked at me and I saw the anger in his eyes.

"Please don't," was all I could muster before he flew at me, pushed me right off my chair, dragged me by my hair into the next room, and kicked me in the stomach. His mom was there as well as his cousin, but they were not going to help. It was the dead of winter and we were six miles out of town. His mom and cousin stayed in the other room.

"Please stop." I cried, but that only made him madder. He choked me. I kicked him as hard as I could and he went flying. I jumped up, ran to the phone, and called the police. I frantically told them I needed help. Hearing him approach, I dropped the phone really fast, hoping he hadn't seen. His mom came in and tried to calm him down, but he wouldn't. He punched me in the face. I went flying and hit the ground. Finally, I saw the lights from the police car pull up.

"You called the cops? Why did you do that!" Heath started panicking. The police came in and I ran to them.

"Please take me and my girls out of here!"

They looked at me and asked, "What's going on?"

I told them and they asked his mom for verification.

"I didn't see anything."

They asked his cousin.

"I didn't see anything."

I shook my head in disbelief. They took Heath out to the police car. About ten minutes later, another police car pulled up and two police officers walked into the house.

"Beatrice, you're under arrest," one of them said.

"What?" I couldn't believe my ears. "Why?"

"You have warrants from Edmonton for unpaid fines."

"What about my girls?"

They asked Heath's mom to watch them. I couldn't find my boots, so they grabbed Heath's rubber boots and threw them at me. "Put these on." They handcuffed me and escorted me to the car.

In the cell, I sat there crying and combing my fingers through my hair as gently as I could. The goose eggs on my head hurt, but not as much as this whole circumstance hurt. After I braided my hair, I began to cry harder. The ball of hair Heath had pulled out of my scalp had been as large as a softball and there was a big bald spot above my forehead.

A few hours later, a police officer came to check on me. "Well, you sure look different from when you first got picked up," she said.

"Yeah, because last night I was beat up and dragged by my hair all over the house." I began to sob uncontrollably but managed to say, "I called the police for help and you took me from my girls. How do I know they're safe?"

The officer reassured me that Heath would not get out of jail. They allowed me to call his sister, someone I absolutely trusted, to ask her to pick up the girls. I spent ten days in a cell.

∞

After I was let out, I ran back to Regina with my girls. I found out that I was a few months pregnant but I kept this to myself. I didn't want to be part of Heath's life anymore. At the age of 28, I gave birth to my eighth child, my baby Jalea. She was my easiest birth and an adorable baby.

My four girls and I lived alone, but I was living an addicted lifestyle again. However, my cupboards were full and my babies were well cared for. I spent my days with my girls, being the best mom I could be. But at night, I partied in all the wrong ways, with all the wrong people, and slept little. Then it happened — someone called Social Services and the police on me again. I fought them off for a while, and then I gave up.

After I lost my four girls to Social Services, I did nothing but drink and stay high, sometimes for three days at a time. I was a stone-cold drunk and druggie. I hated going to sleep because I needed drugs as soon as I opened my eyes or I would be deathbed sick. I needed a downer to put me to sleep and an upper to wake me up; sometimes I bought people's personal methadone.

One morning, I woke up and I didn't have anything to take. I lay in bed feeling so sick I couldn't move. I felt like I was going to die. I was shaking on the inside. I was hot and sweating. My heart beat so slowly it felt like it was going to stop. Thankfully, there was a knock at the door. A friend was here with a slam. I'd be better in a minute. My friend came in and looked at me.

"Oh my God, you need this." She went to the kitchen to prepare our shots. I heard her, and my heart beat fast in anticipation. Minutes seemed like hours. I jumped up and got sick. *What the hell am I doing to myself?* Finally, my friend was ready for me and a minute later I felt better. I wasn't high. I was just not sick. Then, I needed to get ready to make money so I could get high. This was my daily activity. I was in survival mode, but I didn't want to feel like that anymore.

∞

I hid my drugs well so my friend who was staying with me didn't steal them while I was sleeping. I hated this cycle, but I couldn't see any way out at the time. I was bombarded with self-hatred but had such love for my children. I hoped I had the strength to sober up. I just didn't know how to get out of bed. I heard the buzzing of the alarm clock and had to force myself awake. I went to the washroom and had my shot and got ready to go visit my girls. I truly believed they wouldn't be able to tell that I was high

I had to check in at the Social Services building, so I told them my name, and a security guard led me to an office. There was another guard there and the worker sat at her throne and stared at me, looking a little panicked. I looked at her and laughed. Someone was a little frightened today. I gunned her off with the dirtiest look I could give her. I didn't like her. I didn't want to have anything to do with her, but she had my girls, and I wanted them back. She looked at her papers and picked them up to hand to me. I went to grab them and the male guard stepped closer to me.

"Settle down," I said annoyed that the guards thought I would hurt the worker. I grabbed the papers and the social worker told me my court date. I had two weeks to dummy up if I wanted my girls to come home. I intentionally wanted to scare my worker because I didn't want her to know how much she really scared me. She had my girls and she controlled my every move. I didn't want her to know my fear because I didn't want it used against me.

∞

No matter how high I got, I couldn't stop the loneliness in my heart. The silence in the house was killing me. I missed my girls' laughter. I missed hugging them and telling them I loved them. I wanted to cry, but the tears were dried up from my previous days of sorrow. Oh, how I wished my kids were with me, so I could cook them supper. I loved them. I knew I did. So, when the police told me how undisciplined I was for using drugs in my house while there were kids in it, I thought about the ways I made sure my children were okay: how I got them up for school every day, how they were fed and clothed, how I played with them and coloured with them, and how I hugged them and always told them I loved them. I did everything in my power to be a great mom, except for the drugs. Drugs controlled my nights when they were sleeping. As I sat there feeling sad, angry, and full of emotions, I wondered if the girls were sleeping. I wondered if they were together. Oh, how I missed them.

I forced myself to sleep. I thought I was dreaming of Desirae. She was six years old and in Grade 1. I heard a knock at my bedroom window.

"Mommy, open up, Mommy," I heard her say faintly. It felt real. "Mommy, Mommy, I'm here."

I opened my eyes and the knocking continued. I looked up at the window and I saw Desirae's shadow through the curtain.

"Mommy, Mommy, it's me, Desirae."

I jumped up and ran to the front door. I flung it open and I saw her and I grabbed her.

"Oh, my baby girl, how did you get here?" I said through my tears.

"I walked here from school, Mommy. I wanted to see you."

I held her and rocked her. I felt so complete, but fear entered me. What would they do when they saw she was missing? I didn't want to take her back to school, but I knew I had to. I just wanted to keep her with me. My heart broke. I didn't want to give her up again. The first time was hard, but I couldn't let her go again.

"I want to stay with you Mommy, please. Okay?"

"I want you to stay, but you have to go back to school. You need to go back and help with your sisters. You are not alone. I'm here. I love you, my daughter." I walked Desirae back to school, holding in my sadness. I didn't want her to know this was killing me inside.

∞

My life on the streets haunted me. When I felt I had no other way to get money, I would turn back to the old me — that person I could not stand to look at in the mirror. Swollen, black-encircled eyes, hair frizzy with too much product in it; skinny, pale-skinned body, wrapped in the sexiest clothes I could find. My eyes told the story of the haunting pain and loneliness inside me. My anger shed light on my deep hate for the world and everyone in it.

I couldn't look at myself in the mirror because when I saw myself, I saw ugliness and imperfection. I would sit for hours, trying to pick the blemishes from my face. Oh, I hated looking in the mirror. I couldn't stand prostitution. All of it was ugly to me — the sex, the money, the men who opened their wallets. I would see their families' pictures in them. That disgusted me.

I just couldn't settle down. I kept living a destructive lifestyle. *How could I lose all of my children to Child Welfare?* All I could think about was what a failure I was. I was nothing. I was sick and gross and I deserved everything that had happened to me. I had become that drunken man on the corner that Jomaine had pointed to all those years ago when she said, "That's probably your uncle." She was right. I had become that stupid Indian, only worse.

I carried on my destructive lifestyle until I got to the point where I could not get out of bed unless someone brought me drugs. When I woke up, I would rush as fast as I could to the bathroom and dry heave. There was nothing in my stomach. I couldn't even keep water down. I was always freezing and sweating or hot with chills. I couldn't imagine brushing my hair or changing my clothes. I couldn't move, and when I slept, the dreams were terrifying. I had given up on myself and felt my life wasn't worth living.

I tempted death and took too many drugs. Broken, I believed that I actually deserved the hell that I'd been told I was going to burn in. I went to the bathroom and got my drugs ready. I put in double what I would usually take without thinking much of it. I began to inject myself with it but stopped midway. *This is your last chance.* Before the high kicked in, I injected it all. I remember my hand falling to my side and the needle dropping on the floor.

"Oh my God, this is it," was all I could remember saying as my heart pounded frantically. Everything started spinning at a hundred miles an hour. I tried to stand up; I couldn't. I tried to breathe and my eyes rolled back. Suddenly, it was like a movie of my whole life played in my mind. It played real fast and I saw my kids looking at me.

"*No,*" I yelled to myself. "You didn't go through your entire life like this for nothing! There has to be a reason!" I forced myself to stand up and dragged myself to the door. "You're not gonna die! You're not gonna die!" I managed to open the door and then fell down the stairs. I could barely stand up, but I made it into the middle of the street before I fell to my knees. I couldn't keep my eyes open. I felt hands on my shoulders, shaking me, and I heard someone yelling, "Beatrice, Beatrice!"

When I came to, I saw my neighbour, Judy, standing across from me at her dining room table. She looked pissed. Judy was a short, feisty, smart woman whom I and my girls adored. She might have been small, but by the way she was looking at me, I could tell she'd had enough of me. She said something that would change my life.

"Beatrice, you have a choice. "You either choose your kids or you choose your drugs, but you can't have both."

When she said that, it was like someone had stabbed me in the heart. Now when I think about it, it seems like common sense, but she spoke the truth so bluntly. *How could I choose drugs over my kids?*

I didn't say anything. I just got up and walked across the street to my house. I'd tried to kill myself without succeeding. I was alive for a reason and I didn't have a clue how, but I was going to change and get better.

I fell to my knees, broke down, and cried. I remembered all my life's mistakes in an instant. When I looked back on my life, I realized the places where I messed up. I'd lost all my children to Social Services, stolen, lied, and cheated. I did all these things in survival mode, but the guilt still stacked up high. I felt guilty that I had aborted one baby, and I felt incredible sadness about losing another. I'd manipulated every situation I was in to get through the day. I thought of the fights I'd gotten into and how I'd never considered my life to be of any value; how I'd put myself in situations where I should have wound up dead. And yet, here I was.

How could I ever get past this crushing despair? I couldn't take it anymore. I looked to the heavens and cried out, "If there's a God, I need your help now!"

Fireworks didn't go off, but something inside me told me everything was going to be okay.

I remembered the Jesus I had learned about when I was younger. I remembered thinking he was there for everyone but me; no one else cared about me so why would God? The reality was, I hadn't thought much about God when I was out on the streets living my life. But now, I felt this longing to reach out to my Creator . . . whoever God was.

∞

I needed to get help because I didn't ever want to be that sick again. It was scary and I was ready to get my children back. I couldn't live like this, knowing I was choosing drugs over my kids. I made the decision to go to detox. I was going to do it for my kids. I called a facility and they had a bed. I was going.

The cab took forever. When I arrived, they asked if I had used in the last day. I said, "No," for fear they wouldn't take me. I'd just taken my last shot and hoped they couldn't tell. I just didn't want to be sick. It was my first time in Regina Detox, a program housed in an old brick house on Dewdney. Who would have known that the detox was there all this time — I'd walked by it so often.

Sitting in the office, a bigger woman with tight, blonde, curly hair pulled out a bunch of paperwork. "This will take about half an hour. We want to know what we're dealing with," she said with a smirk. I smiled awkwardly at her, unsure of the humour. She asked so many questions that at one point I was about to walk out. I started to feel interrogated and annoyed but I remembered I was going to detox for my kids. I didn't want to experience the drug-induced night life anymore. I wanted my children back. I missed being a mom.

"Beatrice," she said, snapping me back to reality. "Let me show you your room."

I followed her up the stairs and down the hall. She opened my room door. There was a single bed and a small dresser.

"If you need anything, there will be someone downstairs 24-7." She pointed out where the washrooms were and headed downstairs. I closed the door and sat on the bed, unsure of what the night had to offer. I was scared because I knew what withdrawal felt like, and it hurt, but I needed to do this. I needed to get clean and I needed to do it before I killed myself with drugs.

I had a hard time falling asleep and began to tremor. *It's okay, you'll make it.* When I'd felt like this in the past, I would usually take something to knock me out, but that was not a possibility tonight. I lay there and felt my body begin to hurt. I started to regret my decision.

I must have dozed off because I heard, "Beatrice, are you coming down for breakfast?"

I opened my eyes. My stomach was turning. I was sweating, yet cold.

"No," I moaned.

"Okay." The door closed and I drifted off to sleep once more.

"Beatrice, are you coming down for lunch?"

I opened my eyes. I jumped up and ran to the washroom. For ten minutes, I hugged the toilet and couldn't move. Two staff came in and guided me back to my room.

"I can't do this." I cried. "It hurts so bad." I shook uncontrollably. "Oh God, it hurts." My bones ached from my toes to my head. My body throbbed. It felt like I was dying.

The next day, all I could remember was being taken to the hospital and waking up with an IV hooked up to my arm. I still felt sick but it was more like a pneumonia kind of sick. I asked to use the phone and called a friend to bring me a hit. I couldn't do it anymore. When he came, he fixed me up and I immediately felt better. Nobody noticed. The nurses would check me and let me know I was looking much better, which was ironic because it was the illegal drugs that apparently made me look better. That night, the doctor discharged me and I went back to detox. I decided I would only fix enough so that I wouldn't be sick. It was not the best decision I made that week, but I seriously couldn't handle the withdrawal. I felt so defeated. Was I ever going to be able to quit?

∞

In detox, I made a friend, and a few days in, we decided to leave. It was not like my kids' social workers knew where I was anyways. We left and fixed for a good week. But again, I knew that I needed to clean up. I decided to go on the methadone program. That way, I wouldn't be sick, and at least I would get myself off the harder drugs. Being on methadone meant that every day I needed to go to the clinic and get my cup of "juice." The methadone worked as long as I didn't miss a dose. There was hope. I felt it. A couple of months later, I was no longer an everyday, all-day user of T's and R's and morphine.

∞

I went to visit my girls at the Social Services building. They were so cute. My baby, Jalea, was beginning to walk. Dalreesha was two, Kasheena was three, and Desirae was five. As soon as my daughters saw me, they all ran to me and hugged and loved me, a love I never felt like I deserved. I hugged them back, tears rolling down my cheeks.

"I love you girls so much," I whispered in their ears. *I'm going to fight hard to be a good mom. From now, on my kids come first.*

When the girls walked by the workers, they were so polite, saying, "Excuse me please." They pushed their baby dolls in play strollers and when people moved out of their way, they'd say, "Thank you very much."

The workers would smile. "Your girls are so polite, Beatrice," one of the receptionists said.

I smiled. At least I was doing something right.

As time passed, the worker could not believe how much I had changed. During my previous visits, she made sure a security guard stood on either side of me, for fear I would follow through with my threats and hurt her. This day, though, she drove me to get groceries for my girls. My younger children were coming home.

I am thankful the worker saw the change in me. I fought and I got my four younger girls back within a few months.

∞

I wish I could say that I stopped using immediately, but I didn't. Sometimes, I would use with a friend, Cheryl, who lived across the street. She ended up choosing her boyfriend over her daughter, Jessie, who was about fourteen or fifteen at the time. After Cheryl abandoned her, leaving Jessie alone to live in that house by herself, I looked out for her and brought her to my house to eat. If she was partying, I would go over there and kick everyone out. Then, Jessie would come over and just sit on my steps and we would talk.

WOLF WOMAN:
HEARD ALL OVER THE EARTH

ONE DAY, I was sitting on my front steps, watching my girls play on the grass. I noticed a girl, a neighbour from down the street. She came skipping over and told me she'd gone to youth group. She was so excited.

"You should come to church with me," she said.

I stopped her real fast. "You'll never get me through the church doors. I would surely burn."

But every week, she would skip over and beg me to come to church. Finally, one day, to get her off my back, I agreed. The next Sunday she was nowhere to be found, but I packed up my girls and walked to the church half a block away. When I walked through the doors, I was so relieved to find I didn't burst into flames.

I sat down and the service began. My girls aged five and under jumped up and ran wild. They ran through the worship singers and tripped over cords. Once I was finally able to grab them, we left, even though it was during the service. I was so embarrassed. But something drew me back the next week, and the same thing happened. The girls ran wild and I left. I decided to give it one more go but told myself this would be the last time I set foot in those doors. If my girls went all crazy again, I would leave and never return.

This time, the girls didn't even let me sit down. Not only were they running, they were screaming and their arms were going in all directions. I tried to grab them, but try catching four little girls at once. That was not happening I felt so embarrassed and I grew angry. I sat in a chair, waited for them to run my way, and instead they ran by one of the pastors. He scooped two of them up and the other two came running to me.

I looked at him and he said, "It's okay,"

I stayed for church that day.

The next week, I left the girls with my neighbour and I went to church by myself. As the pastor spoke, it felt like he was talking directly to me. I felt really uncomfortable. I would look around to see if it was just me feeling this way. The next week, I went back, and again, I swore he was talking directly to me. Something was tugging at my heart and I couldn't explain it. It was crazy. He kept talking.

I don't remember most of what he said but I do remember him saying, "If you want to accept Jesus into your heart, put your hand up." I felt really nervous and excited and wanted to put my hand up so bad. But I couldn't. Then he said, "I know there's someone in here today who is ready to take this step. Everyone put your heads down. Whoever wants someone to come and pray, will you put your hand up?"

Before I knew it, my hand went up. I had to look at it to make sure it was really up, and that day, I accepted Jesus into my heart. I remember feeling this peace, maybe even relief. That day, I chose God. And although I didn't realize it, long before, God had chosen me. I fought with the idea that someone could love me after everything I'd gone through and everything I'd done. After changing my life around, I experienced miracle after miracle in my life. I realized that even though I'd lived in darkness for so many years, God was still watching over me.

∞

While my older kids were still in the system, I enrolled in university because I wanted to become a reporter and give myself and my kids a future. I started in the adult entrance program. I was so thankful I had my GED.

My days started early. I had the girls up at 6 a.m. When winter came, I would bundle them up and put Kash and Dal in the stroller. I would have Jalea in the carrier and Des would bravely walk beside me, jumping in the stroller when it got too hard for her to walk. Sometimes, the double stroller would be too hard to push through the deep snow. I walked by the community centre where there was a police detachment, and sometimes I would see a woman police officer, watching me and smiling.

Still a little hood, I would gun her off and ask her, "What are you staring at?" This happened for about a week and then she called me in one afternoon when I was walking home after an early class. I hesitated because I had some pretty messed up experiences with police officers and I honestly didn't know if I could trust her. I walked into the community centre. Right away, she asked me where I went every day.

"What's it to you? Am I doing something wrong?" I asked defensively.

"No, not at all." She smiled. "While I'm at work, I see you walk back and forth with your kids and I notice you push a stroller through the snow. That must be hard."

"Yes, it is." I opened up. "I'm a single mother, trying real hard to get my life back in order. I go to university."

"How would you feel if the other officers and I bought you a sled? It would make life much easier on you and your kids."

I looked at her and questioned her motive. *Why would she want to do this for me? What will she get out of it? Is this a set-up?* I couldn't figure it out, so I straight up asked, "Why would you do this for us?"

She smiled. Maybe she was reading my mind. She looked me straight in the eyes and said, "Not all of us are bad."

I took a deep breath, and I don't know why it was so hard to say, but I managed to squeak out a "Sure," and walked away.

∞

A week later, while I was walking by, the policewoman called me in to the station. A long blue sled with a bow on it stood between two police officers. I honestly didn't know how to respond.

"This is for you and your girls." She also handed me a $50 Hudson's Bay gift card. "We see what you're doing for your family and we just want to encourage you with these gifts. Nothing more, nothing less."

"Thank you. I don't know what else to say."

"You don't have to say anything at all. Knowing that we helped to make your walk a little easier is thanks enough."

∞

At this time, I was living in North Central Regina, a crime-laden neighbourhood. Not surprisingly, this provided all kinds of triggers that taunted me daily. I ended up getting a low-income house in the north end of the city and moved there with my four girls.

On day, while washing the dishes and staring out the kitchen window at the open field, I prayed, "Creator, please, can I see my older children? I miss them so much." Tears streamed down my face. I braved the call to the social worker and, without any hesitation, she said she would bring them down for an overnight visit later that week. I put the phone down. I was shaking! After all these years, they were going to let me visit my babies. Well, they definitely weren't babies anymore — they were ten, twelve and thirteen years old. Wow.

I didn't tell my younger ones in case it didn't happen. I didn't look forward to anything in case there was a chance of being let down. Friday took forever to come. The week dragged on. Getting to university every day sure took everything I had. I would leave at 6 a.m. with my four girls, catch the bus to the daycare, drop them off, and get back on the bus to school. Some days, I wouldn't get home until suppertime, but I was determined not to give up.

Friday arrived and I sat on the couch, unable to sit still, jumping up, pacing back and forth, looking out the window, and sitting down. Finally a car pulled into my driveway. *I see them, I see them.* My heart beat frantically. *Oh my gosh. Will they like me? Will they know I've wanted to see them all this time?* I watched them pile out of the car and I ran to the door.

I called my younger girls to come. "Hurry, I want you to see someone!" The girls came running, screaming, chasing each other.

"Who, Mamma? Who?"

"Your brothers and sister."

They looked at me, puzzled, and ran to the door. I opened it, and there stood the worker and my children. They were so shy and wouldn't look at me.

"Come in," I motioned. They followed me in and sat on the couch. The girls jumped all over them and definitely were not shy. All I could do was stare at them and smile as tears rolled down my face. It was a miracle having them sit in my living room. God had answered my simple prayer, and I believe to this day my Creator had heard the cries of my mother's heart. I was so thankful.

∞

During the weekend, my children started warming up to me. We talked and laughed for hours. My oldest son asked me if I could talk to him in private and he began to tell me of the awful abuse they'd been facing in the foster home. I couldn't leave them there so I called the Regina workers and we got my older babies out of there as fast as we could. I refused to let the foster parents pick up my kids. My children ended up going to another foster home where they were safe. We had regular visits, and soon after that, my children came home. My life was complete — well, just about complete.

I met my husband, Fergus, through church. A year later, when we were planning our wedding, I longed for the touch of a mom. I wished for her love, something I had never experienced and never would. The mother "love" given to me was forced — Jomaine may have loved me but I never felt it.

Now, in my thirties, I tried to make amends in my relationship with Jomaine so I could have a parent at my wedding. She was the only parent I had ever known, and I wanted her to be there. I wanted to forgive her and move forward with my life, possibly with her in my life. We met and had a few visits, and one day, I told her I was so sorry for the way I'd acted when I was on the streets. I'd been angry and blamed her for my being there and that was wrong. She apologized to me too, but she also let me know that she'd adopted me because she felt pressured to. She didn't want me. She'd felt guilty.

I tried to make sense of it, but I couldn't. It hurt to have been taken from my mom and given to a mom that didn't even want me. The worst of it was that I'd never experienced a dad. People wonder why I'm messed up. I didn't experience a mom; I never knew a dad.

Our family was together. There were ten of us: Fergus and me plus my 7 children and Fergus's daughter, all between the ages of two and fifteen years old. Life was crazy, to say the least. We lived in a three-bedroom, mouse-infested house that was way too crowded, but we had so much fun. We had dance-offs and singing contests, and we played hide and seek. I would be right in there, because it was as though I was growing up with the kids, like I was a teenager again. I was still rough around the edges and still very street in the way I interacted with my children and with people in general, but I promise I was trying.

∞

At this time, I realized I needed to deal with my outstanding warrants before I got picked up by police. I had a long record, mostly thefts, assaults, and failures to appear in court. I turned myself in and the police let me out and gave me a court date. I went to court and the judge told me to get legal representation because she was looking at giving me two years plus a day, which meant I would be going to the women's penitentiary.

I spoke with Spurgeon, one of the pastors of my church, who was by then a good friend of mine, and told him what was going on. He and his wife asked if they could come to court with me, and I agreed.

I got all my affairs in order and was ready to do my time, hoping that if all went well, I would be out in a year. My husband and my church family were going to look after my children. I knew they would be in good hands.

"Mommy will be back as soon as I can. I love you all so much." Tears ran down from my eyes. My family had been complete for over a year, but I had to do my time for my crimes. I had been caught with $1000 worth of stolen mall merchandise when I was in addiction, and I'd failed to go to court at the time. That charge was over two years old and it had never been dealt with.

My children hugged me and cried, but I had to go. I had to be free of all my charges so I could get on with my life.

∞

Spurgeon and his wife came to court with me and as we waited for my legal representative, Spurgeon asked if he could pray for me.

I said, "What?" Looking around, I wondered what people would think. "I don't know . . . Is that something you people do?"

He laughed and said, "Yeah, I can pray quietly."

"Go ahead, then."

Spurgeon prayed, then I went to talk to the lawyer. He stated straight out what jail time I was looking at and asked if I had my legal stuff in order.

Since my last name started with a W, I was one of the last people called. "Beatrice Wallace," the judge finally called. Not that I was in a rush to go to jail, but finally. I walked up to the front and listened to my charges. After the judge looked at me, she asked if I had anything to say.

"Yes, your Honour. These charges are a couple of years old and since then, I've become a recovering addict. I was into hard drugs at the time and my children were in care. Since then, I have cleaned up, am on the methadone program, put myself into university and all seven of my children are out of care. They all live with my husband and I, and my step-daughter. I have a church family and have been working on myself so I will never be in that place in my life again."

The judge looked up at me over her glasses. She studied me for a long time. "Do you have anyone here with you?"

"Yes, I have my pastor and his wife. She was my maid of honour." I turned and looked at them and they waved.

"Because of your record, I was definitely looking at giving you time."

"Yes, your Honour. I understand."

There was the longest pause ever. She slowly took off her glasses and stared at me. "I hereby give you eighteen months . . . eighteen months' probation."

I couldn't believe my ears. I turned around and looked at Spurgeon. Was it his prayer that had changed the judge's mind? I was baffled.

"Thank you. Thank you so much!" I cried.

"Don't make me regret this decision. And good luck on your journey. It looks like you're on the right path. Keep it up."

∞

When things got rough, I would still take off for a night and go party and drink. I tried to stay clean by being on the methadone program. It helped with the drug cravings, but my mind was still so messed up. After a year and a half, I ended up taking time off from university because I couldn't manage my home, children, and going to school.

I realized in order to be the best mom I could be, I needed to get off the methadone. I was on a high dose. It slowed me down and I slept a lot. I started to lower my doses, but as soon as I would get down to 40–50 ml, I would start withdrawing, and it caused tremendous pain in my whole body. I went up and down with my doses for a couple of months, and finally, when I was at 30 ml, I decided to just stop, cold turkey, with support from my husband. I did stop, but I do *not* recommend that method to anyone. The pain and the sickness I experienced was unbearable. There were times when I just about went back on, but no, I toughed it out, and about ten days later, I started feeling better.

Then, I fell into a deep depression, which I found hard to fight. I was told I had developed drug-induced bipolar disorder. The diagnosis totally made sense to me because some days I was flying off the walls and the next few days, I would be lying in my bed, feeling suicidal. It was a hard journey. I'd kicked the drugs, but drinking was harder to stop. I didn't drink nearly as much as I had before but enough that I would act up and regret it the next day. Our family was doing well. The boys were graduating from Grade 12, and everyone was moving up a grade.

∞

There were a few things that I asked God for. "Please, please, don't let any of my children experience sexual exploitation or the harsh gang life. And, Creator, I pray they will all finish high school and not become young teen parents." So far, so good. Most parents would not even consider praying these prayers, but I knew the damage that each of those experiences had done to me, and I could not bear for my children to experience any of them.

Before I was completely off drugs, I ended up getting my first job at a computer place where I was introduced to some amazing, decent people. They walked with me on my journey. The wife and daughter of the company's owner took me to buy a woman's suit. I remember being in the store, trying on this outfit, and it was totally not me, but I felt so sophisticated when I wore it. I felt special, maybe deserving of a different life. I also worked in a retirement home. I kept myself busy with two jobs and raising eight children.

∞

After a couple of years of living in that beat-up house, we were given a brand spanking new, five-bedroom house with two bedrooms on the top floor and three on the bottom. The upstairs had an open concept, and I didn't want a TV there because that was our family area. It was and is a beautiful home.

We helped build our home through Habitat for Humanity. As part of the agreement, my kids and I, and whoever else wanted to help, put in 500 hours of work equity as our down payment. Often we would work in the ReStore, sorting through paint or putting blinds in pairs. There was a lot to do in this warehouse, but my kids and I always made the most of that time by finding ways to make our work fun. We were so happy to be spending time together. One thing my three older kids and I would do was pretend to make music videos or make a scary movie. Sometimes there were up to sixteen of us together. We always made the most of our time together. We always had fun.

∞

My only concern about the house was that it was back in the hood. Would I be able to handle this? I had stopped using intravenous drugs for a couple of years by then, but as soon as I moved back to the hood, the cravings got intense. I started dreaming about using and would wake up feeling high. One day, I was staring across the street where a known drug dealer lived. I was looking towards the house thinking *no one will know if I go over there and have a shot.* Our house was clean, supper would be made

— nobody would know. But then, I thought of my kids and, although my heart was pounding intensely, I knew I couldn't go over there. I knew I wouldn't. But I hated the cravings.

I stared right at the drug dealer's house. I looked and prayed, "God, please take these cravings away. I don't want to use drugs. That would be the worst decision I could make at this time. But the cravings won't stop. I can't stand the hard beating of my heart, to the point where I feel like I am going to choke on it. I can't do this. I am asking you, with everything I have in me, to *please* take these cravings away."

Suddenly, I saw the dealer standing on his porch, and the next thing I knew, I had a vision of myself standing on one side of him and my old best friend on the other side. We were giggling, throwing our heads back, laughing a simple laugh. This is what we call "marking someone in." We were saying everything to please him and flirting up a storm. This went on for several minutes, and finally we all went inside. I gasped, "*No.* I didn't want to go inside." I didn't want to take drugs.

That's when I heard as plain as day, "I heard your cry. You are healed."

To this day, I have never had a craving for drugs again. That is how good our Creator is.

∞

After years of struggling, I was committed to my healing journey, one that would open up some of the wounds I have shared here. I trusted that my Creator would be there beside me, and sometimes I would need to be carried because of the brokenness of my inner being. I was able to forgive my adoptive mom and all those people who had hurt me. I sought forgiveness from the people I had wronged, and I still seek reconciliation. I cried out to the Creator many times. The pain was so unbearable. All I could do was weep and I felt consoled. Sometimes when I forgot and tried to struggle through life myself, the Creator would gently remind me that I was loved.

I heard this whisper in my ear. "You've come through much pain and sorrow, but it doesn't have to continue. Just listen to the whisper in your ear. I am so proud of you, for how far you've come. I love you, Beatrice."

∞

I was starting to feel like a different person. There was a lot to fight inside of me, though, and thinking back, I wish I'd sought out healing with a more deliberate approach. For so many years, I battled my scars by using substances and being in abusive relationships. When the time came that I was not high or drunk on a daily basis, my emotions sometimes got the best of me. I was easily triggered by a smell, a sound, or a person. I was angry. I was sad. I was way crazy happy. My emotions controlled me. I experienced immobilizing panic attacks. Three of the worst ones chased me back to nights of using drugs. I cried for no reason and burst out with anger when triggered. I was a mess, but I was healing. It was just really slow.

I was trying to be in tune when my Creator would speak to me. We shared extremely beautiful and intimate experiences. I know I'm fortunate because people often tell me they can see it.

∞

One day, I was sitting and thinking about the devastating year that White Bear First Nation had experienced. There had been thirty-five unnatural deaths there like homicides, suicides and drug overdoses. God placed a burden on my heart. I wondered what could be done. A thought came into my head. I closed my eyes and pictured people joining me, including members of the reserve, praying throughout the reserve. God emphasized that we wouldn't be alone.

After that thought, I felt a sense of urgency. I called my friend Nick, another pastor at my church, and told him and his wife, Vivian, what I had experienced. His wife was also from White Bear and she began to cry. Excitedly and through their tears, they explained to me that the picture I'd see was a vision from God. I felt an overwhelming joy.

We prayed and committed to following through with what God had shown me in my vision. We had our first prayer walk of many. What an awesome honour and experience it was for me, a girl from the hood, to be used by God.

∞

It was an early morning drive to White Bear that took two-and-a-half hours. Through the windows, we could see a storm dancing in the sky. The winds were picking up and raindrops started to drizzle as fear entered my heart. It beat a mile a minute, but I trusted that this was not of me but of God. We all piled out of our vehicles. There were about sixty of us — leaders from the reserve had anticipated what God was going to do. It was an extremely high expectation.

The night before, we had gathered in my house and made colourful signs. Children and adults laughed and enjoyed being together. I explained my vision, and refreshing tears flowed down my face.

Standing on the reserve, I gazed at the coming storm and I prayed, "Dear God, let this storm pass." We began walking. Indigenous Christian music played from the van that led the group of walkers. As I walked up the driveway towards the highway, I felt this indescribable tug at my heart, as if God was saying, "Thank you for trusting Me and being obedient."

At the start of the walk, the sun blazed and there was a sprinkle of warm rain from the heavens. The storm that had been coming in our direction stopped right in front of us and gracefully moved around us, not disturbing us a bit.

I looked at the pastor walking beside me. "Did you see that?" I asked.

His eyes widened with hope and his smile brightened. Again, a tear escaped my eye.

We felt God's presence throughout the whole four-kilometre walk. We sang and we prayed. We laughed and we cried. People driving by honked in support and stopped to thank us. Some joined us mid-walk as we passed their property. At the end of the walk, we shared music, a testimony, a potluck meal and a barbeque, and we finished with a giveaway. We enjoyed being in community by the lake.

I took a minute and walked towards the lake to gaze upon Creator's greatness and was thankful for being able to fulfill this vision. I was still in awe that this happened.

∞

A few weeks after the walk, I got a call from my biological sister, Patti, who was only thirteen months older than me. We met again, for the first time since my 5th birthday party. I absolutely adored her. She was my best friend in an instant. I loved hanging with her. She made me feel happy and safe. We don't talk as much as I would like to, but when you're ripped apart at a young age, you lose that time to bond. That's why I would get so upset at my children when they fought, because I never wanted them to be apart again. I wanted them to always be there for each other, forever. My brother, Vince, ended up moving back to Regina, and we reconnected too. I found out that two of my other siblings, Madeline and Rick, lived in Vancouver.

∞

Sometime later, I started as a volunteer at Soul's Harbour Rescue Mission. I saw that they wanted a paid cook for the soup kitchen, so I applied. My winning remark was, "Well if I can cook for ten people, I'm sure I can cook for two hundred." They hired me on the spot.

At the soup kitchen, I began to run into people from my past. The first time I saw my old drug dealer, Todd, I was paralyzed with fear. He was looking at me. *Should I talk to him? Should I avoid him?* I was shaking so much I needed to put down a tray of food before I dropped it. One of the volunteers touched me on my arm. I jumped. She snapped me out of the memories his presence triggered.

"Where did you go?" She giggled.

I scanned the room once again. There were over a hundred people there, some slurping on their soup, some serving, some laughing, some with heads bowed down in shame. I couldn't hear anything. I spotted Todd once more. He was super skinny. His curly hair had thinned out and he looked sickly. Because I still bumped into people I used to use with, I knew his girlfriend had died from HIV a few months before. It looked like he was facing the same fate.

He looked up at me and our eyes connected. My heart beat frantically and the room spun. I knew what was about to happen. This was not the first time I'd had a panic attack. I started praying, "Lord let me make it to the washroom. Oh, Lord, please!" I walked past the serving trays, touching the wall for guidance. *Beatrice you're going to be okay. You're strong. You're going to make it.*

I turned the corner. *Twenty more steps and you'll be safe.* I touched the door and felt the freedom of no longer having to hold it together. I shut the door and slid against the wall to the floor and started hyperventilating. *Breathe! Breathe! You're going to be OK!* I shook and rocked uncontrollably. I grabbed my knees and screamed quietly but forcefully from the depth of my belly. I'm not sure how long this went on, but a knock at the door snapped me out of it.

"You okay in there?"

And that was it. I shook it off, got up, looked at myself in the mirror, and told myself, "You got this." *God help me.*

"Coming," I answered. I checked my hands and they were not shaking as badly as they'd been earlier. *One more hour and you go home.*

Since this was not my first panic attack, I knew what was happening, and I knew that as long as I could get myself to a safe, quiet place, I could work through it. Was it exhausting? Heck yeah. But I worked in a place where I was met with my past life on the daily. I was not scared of my old dealer, but a flood of emotions attacked me all at once and were unbearable. I prayed that night that I wouldn't have daily triggers. It obviously wasn't that easy though.

∞

About a week later, I was standing at the door when Todd walked in again. Sometimes I liked to greet our guests and joke with them. Some would ask, "What's for supper tonight?" and I would jokingly say, "Food." It got to the point where no one would ask me anymore because they knew the answer. After my famous joke, I looked at the next person coming in and found Todd smiling at me.

"Beatrice, how's it going?"

I froze, but only for a brief second. "I'm doing good. I'm clean now," I blurted out.

"Happy for you," he said and walked to take his seat. Something in me released, maybe a bond I had developed with him because of the control I'd given him as a drug dealer. I felt a sense of freedom. I had taken a piece of Beatrice back.

That night as I lay in my bed, recounting the growth I'd experienced that day, I prayed. "I know that everything I've gone through in my life was for a reason. I want to use my life's experience to help people, especially women like my Indigenous sisters who have experienced what I have in my life." I prayed, "God, use me as you see fit." I slept well that night. It was as if God had heard my heart and was preparing me to start using the gifts and talents I'd been given at birth.

I decided that if I was going to work with vulnerable people, I would need to stop drinking. Up until this point, I would still drink once every couple of months, and sometimes monthly. But I wanted to be an example, so I quit.

∞

I worked at the soup kitchen for a couple of years and it changed so much during that time. When I first started, there were fights every second night. Now, there was no fighting. It even had a family atmosphere. When someone would come in drunk, I would let them sit at the table closest to the door. I would warn them, "If you act up, you will be escorted out" and I kept my word. I was not too shy to roll up my sleeves and guide them out the doors. It happened on a few occasions, so people knew I was serious.

I served the same crowd, month after month. I felt myself getting to the place where I was annoyed and testy. I wasn't sure where that was coming from. Then one day, I spoke the words, "Gosh, will they never change?" I felt fed up. Every night I shared a fifteen-minute devotion and prayer. This night was no exception, but my heart wasn't in it.

After making sure the spaghetti was ready to be served, I stood in front of the guests. For a brief moment, I recalled my week. Suddenly, my heart hurt. It hurt so much that I grabbed my chest and my face crumpled at the agony. I caught my breath as I looked around the room. It was as though God was allowing me to see everyone's pain. I looked at one of our guests. His long, grey hair stood up, going every which way, and his beard looked like it had not been maintained for a long time. His navy overalls smelled like urine and were stained from being worn for weeks. My heart connected with his heart, and for a second, I felt his pain. It hurt. It felt exactly like mine. Although we probably experienced very different lives, his pain still felt the same as mine.

I scanned the room. The pain was so visible and God told me, "I made you strong, and unfortunately some people don't know their strength. That is why I brought you here." I felt peace and love at that very moment.

That evening, I explained to the guests what had happened only minutes prior. I told them, "I'm no better than you. We are all made equal. Our God wants us to know our worth and that we are loved, even when we don't feel it." I learned such a powerful lesson that night.

∞

Fergus and I were married for fifteen years and, although we are not together anymore, I thank God for all that we did together. We grew and worked through so much. To work through the disappointment of my failed marriage, I processed my feelings by writing a letter that I never sent.

Dear Fergus,

> *I should have told you that I was insecure when we were to be married. I sure put on a good show — a strong, independent woman who feared nothing. I had just begun life in recovery and had many secrets that I could not share because shame would have devoured me. You see, when I became a Christian, I prayed to God, "Please let me be with someone." My requirements were very slim. One, he was to never have been in jail. Two, he could not be a gangster who used drugs. Three, he had to have a job and a car. But, most importantly, he had to accept my seven children. Well, you fit these requirements. So one evening, I told you everything, hoping you would leave, but you didn't. I decided to try and fall in love with you. Through my insecurities, I would heal a bit and then run to the streets. You stuck with me and helped me raise my children.*

I also realized your insecurities and unfortunately, we both thrived in our brokenness. And here we are today, fifteen years later, separated. But they were not wasted years — they were years of growing and healing, none of which I regret. We are better friends than lovers. And there was way more to it than that.

∞

After two years as a cook at Soul's Harbour, I was promoted to emergency services manager. One day, while I was sitting at my desk, I received a phone call.

"You might not remember me, but my name is Glendyne, and I met you when my church and I were serving at the soup kitchen. I would love to take you out to lunch so I can speak to you about something."

Without thinking about it too much, I said, "Sure." I love food, and it's rare that I turn down an opportunity to eat. When I started university, I introduced myself to Strawberry CheeseQuake Blizzards at Dairy Queen. My oh my, that was my daily treat, and my growing waist sure proved my love for food.

The next week, Glendyne picked me up and we went to The Diplomat Steakhouse. That was the fanciest restaurant I'd ever been to. She explained to me that she was starting Defend Dignity, an initiative to end sexual exploitation through awareness, advocacy, and aid. As she spoke, I started to feel shame. This topic was something I'd never talked about to anyone. *Does she know? Should I tell her?* I remembered praying to God that I would be used in some way to help my Indigenous sisters. *Is this the answer to my prayer?*

Without a thought, I explained, "Except for my husband, I have never talked about this to anybody. I've carried this with me all these years. I was a prostitute at thirteen years old." When I said that, shame filled me and tears escaped my eyes. I didn't want to look at her because I was hoping deep down that she would not judge me. When I looked up at her, she had tears in her eyes. I felt such a weight lifted off me. I cried even harder. I had held this secret close to my heart for so long, in fear of judgment, in fear of being ridiculed, and in fear of being reminded what a dirty little girl I was. I told Glendyne about my days on the street, and I will never forget what she said. "It wasn't your fault. You were just a little girl."

I had never looked at it like that. I had always been so ashamed because I was the one standing on the street corner and I was the one taking the money from the johns. I remembered, in the beginning, I handed the money over to pimps. I didn't think of them as pimps back then, but now I know that when a man is taking money from a girl after she has sex with a john, he is a pimp. And when the girl is underage, she is being sexually exploited.

Through my work with Defend Dignity, I learned that sexual exploitation is the sexual abuse of children and youth through the exchange of sex or sexual acts for drugs, food, shelter, protection, money, and other basics needs of life. I had been exploited many times over and realized I'd been taken advantage of because of my vulnerability as a young homeless person who was highly reliant on drugs.

I joined the Defend Dignity team, and it was one of the biggest times of growth in my life. I met other sexually exploited survivors with brave voices. I listened to them speak openly about what they'd gone through, and they amazed me with their courage. Within the year, I began using my voice as well, speaking mostly at churches, but also in schools and at different events across Canada. The shame began to disappear when I finally realized it was not my fault. I had been a victim in my experiences of sexual exploitation.

∞

I worked at Soul's Harbour for a couple more years and they invested in my personal growth as well. I was mentored by a great boss who had a lot of patience with me as I grew into a leader in my community. My home life was amazing. I was sober and my children were growing. Our house was full of laughter and joy. We were a loud family, and I know people would get overwhelmed when they visited because we were all so hyper.

After I quit working at Soul's Harbour, I fell into a depression for a few months and didn't realize I was mourning my old job. I look back on it now and see it as plain as day, but at the time, nope.

I decided I needed to work, so I got a position as a youth mentor and a teacher's aide at a school. Partway through the year, my criminal record came up, and I was told I could finish the year at the school but would then be dismissed. The principal fought for me to stay there, but at the same time, the administration was worried about "what the parents would think" when they found out about my past. I got it.

I then got a job at a non-profit organization called Aids Programs South Saskatchewan (APSS) that worked with people with or at risk of getting HIV or AIDS. APSS had a needle exchange for intravenous drug users, and this would be the first time I had ever touched a needle since the time I was using them myself. I really prayed through it. I remember the first time working in the needle exchange, I shook when giving people their needles, but after a week, I was okay.

One day when I was working, one of my abusers walked in. I froze, recalling one night when I was about fifteen years old and had been awoken with a man on top of me, having sex with me. I had thrown him off.

"What the hell is wrong with you?" I asked. I scrambled to my feet as he ran down the stairs and out the door before I could catch up to him. I had never given it much thought after that, until that day when I saw him again. I couldn't move.

He walked out of the needle exchange room and I walked down the stairs to my office and hid myself in the coffee room. I was shaking uncontrollably. I didn't realize until that moment the effect he'd had on me. All I could do was rock back and forth, holding my legs. I was immobilized.

My boss walked in and asked if I was okay.

I said, "Yeah, I just saw an old abuser."

I went home that night, not fully realizing the effect seeing my abuser had on me. It brought up so many ugly feelings and I couldn't talk about it to anyone. I did the unthinkable and turned to the bottle. After years of being sober, I started drinking. I told myself that I could have a glass of wine, that I could have one drink.

I drank to get drunk. Then it became a habit. Others didn't realize until they saw I was trying to be a social drinker. I got too drunk and ended up freaking out and was charged with assaulting a police officer. That was only after a couple of months of my social drinking "career." I came clean right away with my boss, explained what had triggered me, and shared that the experience had brought up so many ugly feelings that I didn't know how to deal with. I committed to going to counselling, something I'd tried a couple of times before but hadn't found helpful.

∞

I was given nine months' probation because, according the courts, I was doing well in my life. But I was required to see an addictions counsellor and stay sober. Which I did. When I completed the counselling, they gave me a test and informed me I was at risk of reoffending because of my past behaviours, though I thought it was totally unfair to judge me on that basis.

My work at APSS was going well. I would run into old "friends" and dealers who were still living my old lifestyle. I would see some of my extended family coming in to pick up needles. My heart broke for God's people.

One day, I was standing by the receptionist's desk, talking with my two coworkers and my boss, when that same abuser walked in again. I froze again, but this time I locked eyes with my coworker. She looked up at me and I just kept staring. Suddenly, it felt like I was out of my body, watching myself from a distance and seeing how I was interacting with everyone. Everything was in slow motion. I was still staring at my coworker, and she nodded to me as if to say "it's okay."

I snapped out of it and heard my boss say, "What do you think, Beatrice?"

I turned to him and said, "I didn't hear a word you said." I walked into the coffee room and they followed. I guess my boss had spoken for about five minutes, and all that time I had disassociated. This time I knew I had to talk about it. Now, I honestly look at that experience as a gift from God. After that, I was able to recognize when I was being triggered. I did not always handle it properly, but knowing what was happening was a sign of growth.

∞

I worked at APSS for another six months until Fergus and I bought a computer business in Regina. I helped him run the business and ended up taking it over. For a year, I put my blood, sweat, and tears into getting that business to a good place. This was a huge step away from the vulnerable girl who'd been told on many occasions that she would be dead by the time she was thirty. Unfortunately, we went through a lot with this business and as I look back on it now, I realize it broke our marriage. But it didn't break us as people and we are still friends.

∞

I really want to talk about the successes in my life — how I overcame years of addiction, how I overcame homelessness and being lost, and how I overcame just being human, barely surviving on this earth. How God did not let me die by suicide that day, and how he did not let me die of an overdose. How God stopped me from being killed on numerous occasions. I was meant to be here.

I love my relationship with my Creator, and sometimes in my confusion and my brokenness, I still question my existence. But I know that I'm here for a reason, even if it's just to share my story and the wonderful works that have been done in my life. Every day is a blessing for me.

There are days when I am still triggered, and in these moments, there is no way to stop the nightmarish memories. I don't always remember to pray because I am so wrapped up in self-pity. But then I fight through my evil thoughts and I'm able to close my eyes and thank God that I'm free of abuse and I'm a leader in my community.

∞

There are days when I weep for the relationship I once had with my God — the days when I woke up and felt His presence all through the day and when I closed my eyes to sleep. *Where are you now? What's happened? Do you not hear my cries at night? Do you not feel my anguish and my restlessness when I awake in the morning? All day, when I am fighting to survive and I call out to you, do you know the pain I cling to?* And again, I go to bed exhausted. Again, I cry myself to sleep.

What — has — happened?

I knew I had told God to, "use me as you see fit." I remember longing for something, and I found out it was a relationship with God, with my Creator, who would never leave me alone. When I realized the humanity in my pastors and took them off their pedestals, God showed me who I was in a relationship with, and I was not alone.

After my realization, I wrote a journal and spoke to God about my new beliefs.

> *Through it all, I cling to the hope of what was and what is still to come. I know in my heart You did not leave me. It was I who wandered away, and as I try to find my way back, I cling to Your love and Your promise to be there. I cling to the hope that you will never leave me or forsake me. I cling to Your everlasting love. You have said I am valuable so that is what I cling to. You are amazing and You created us all in Your image. What a beautiful thought to cling to in my days going forward.*

I teach my children, and anyone who will listen, that the church is for community, but your relationship with God is the truest gift. I speak with my Creator on the daily, many times, really, and I am shown that I am loved. When we seek a relationship with God, it's much easier to sit in church and truly hear the message that our imperfect pastors desire to get across to us.

Sometimes, it's hard to stay afloat, but I have dreams and desires. I believe my Creator gave me a vision when I was 35 years old and I can see it as plain as day — a ranch for girls and women and their children who have been exploited and need to learn how to live free from shame. A place where they can learn the basics of living and learn how to love themselves and others. But most importantly, a place where they can learn to love themselves as children of God.

∞

Some days, anxiety is only ever a breath away. I constantly self-talk in my car mirror.

"Beatrice, you are going to be okay." I'm not sure what is troubling me — nothing really happened at these moments to set me off — but my heart beats a mile a minute. No matter what I say to myself, it doesn't slow down. *Creator, please help me understand why my anxiety is so high. Please make this nervous feeling go away.* It comes out of nowhere, but I've learned to self-talk and, thankfully, I'm still learning how to deal with these emotions.

Sometimes when my phone rings, my stomach gets in knots and my hands sweat and shake. And sometimes, I just let it go to voicemail. Maybe it's because my ex, Hurbert, will call and greet me with, "Hey, you slut, you should be dead." A few of those calls would explain why I'm nervous to pick up the phone. It hasn't been that bad this year, though. It's getting better through healing and prayer.

I hate how my heart beats a mile a minute, because it makes me lose focus on my goal. My goal is to be whole. My healing journey will be known. If my heart agrees that it will be okay, maybe I won't have to have these talks every day in the front of the mirror.

∞

I am a mother, a kukom (grandma), and an overcomer. When I hold my grandbabies, I'm full of delight. Why was I blessed so? I close my eyes and I feel pure joy. I raised survivors and overcomers. I think back on ten years. I had eight children running around — dysfunction at its finest — but the love, the laughter, and the meals together were such a beautiful sight. I know so much pain in my family's life was not God's intended plan, but I also know that we overcame much, because my children and I trusted in the process.

One time, I was having lunch with some friends and a couple of my girls, and a friend asked, "What is it like to be a kukom?"

I answered, "It's like no other love I have ever felt."

I felt a sting as my daughter, Kasheena, gasped, "What?"

"No, no, I just mean it's a different kind of love. I love you so much but I have to give you a disciplined love."

I can, and do, tell my children about the mistakes I made as a parent, which they can take or not. I've been through it and I learned the hard way, so hopefully they don't have to.

I'm the most perfectly imperfect mother and kukom. I love my tribe so much and I will do everything in my power to help them succeed and be happy in life.

∞

With my eyes closed, I see my future clearly. I see my success and happiness, and life is worth living. The problem occurs when I open my eyes. A tear escapes because it's so darn hard. Trauma-filled lives are not easy to overcome, and when I share my story with others, they sympathize with me and apologize for my hurt. I'm not going for that; I'm looking for change. I look at them. I'm not jealous, or am I? I look around at their successes, their beautiful homes, their spouses and families. I'm not jealous, or am I?

I want their blissful memories, their laughter and their joy, their mom and dad taking them on trips to faraway places, building the memories they show me in their photo albums. I want to open my eyes and be on that exotic island just for a moment, with my own wonderful memories.

Although I don't have what they have, I suppose I shouldn't compare my life to theirs. As I fight to make my own beautiful memories, I need to wipe away the tears. I can see where my tragedy can be made into beauty. I have to keep on the right path. I can make these memories now, with my family. I'm not a lost cause and I have much life left in me. Being on an exotic island could still become my reality.

When I was 40 years old, my family and I went on our first family vacation, to Edmonton. The next year we went to Minnesota. We are making memories that I absolutely cherish. I have a future to look forward to, whereas at one time I didn't. I can see where we are happy and our memories are grand. I'm excited for my future because I do have one. I tell myself not to give up and not to compare because it's unhealthy at best. I'm blessed with eight children and grandbabies galore. I can't wait for their stories to greet me at my door. I'm not jealous; I'm hopeful for the days to come.

∞

In 2016, I started really praying. I was attending a different church and I was struggling with my identity — who was I as a Christian Indigenous woman? I prayed it would be okay for me to find out. Then, over a period of two years, I had interactions with two ladies who were prayer warriors. One told me she saw a vision of me standing in white regalia. God was shooting me out with a bow and arrow, and He said, "I will use you for my people."

I wanted to experience my Indigenous culture, but unfortunately, growing up, I'd been shamed and taught it was wrong and evil. Although, in my heart, I never believed that. I thought, it's just like a religion or culture — I could not believe it was all bad; it just didn't sit with me.

∞

Between 2016 and 2018, many murders happened near my house, four within a one-block radius. I always believed that our house was a lighthouse. Unfortunately, all around my house there were often sirens, fighting, and partying.

One night, I woke up and my daughter, Desirae, had let the next door neighbour into our house. I ran upstairs because my daughter was yelling, "Mom! Mom!" and it scared me. My neighbour was lying on my floor with blood all around him. I shut the door, locked it, grabbed a towel and put pressure on his biggest wound.

"Call 9-1-1!" I yelled. The man was crying.

"She saved me. She saved me," he said.

I looked at Desirae, who was now fifteen.

"He was banging at the door, yelling, 'They're going to kill me. Please open up,'" she said. I couldn't be mad at the danger she'd put herself in. A few days later, he stopped by to thank my daughter for saving his life. I was so proud of her, but I made sure she knew that if there was ever a next time, she should come and get me first.

A few months later, I heard a knock at my door, and I looked out. There was yellow tape across the street and on my yard. A fireman was hosing down red water. A police officer greeted me and asked if I'd heard anything that morning. I hadn't. He explained that there'd been a murder right in front of my car and I would not be able to leave until the firefighter was done his work. That death broke my heart, especially when I found out it was a young woman, not even twenty years old.

A few weeks later, there was another murder just up the street from my house. A lady from our community hosted a Rag Tie Ceremony, where our community gathered to pay respects to people who had been murdered. She wanted to bring awareness to the violence that was happening in North Central Regina. I contacted her to see how I could help.

That evening, there were about 150 people gathered at the ceremony. It was an amazing evening of a community coming together. An elder shared wise words. People from the community who had lost family members to murder shared their experiences, and there was the ceremony itself (which I won't write about, out of respect). The evening ended with a round dance.

A week passed and I couldn't stop thinking about what had happened and how our community was craving change. I made a couple of calls and within the next few days, I and two others gathered in my living room with a sense of urgency. Something had to be done. There was so much violence in our community. Death seemed to greet our doorsteps weekly. We experienced distressed feelings of anticipation as we gathered our thoughts and contemplated what could be done.

We decided on a community gathering to hear what our neighbours desired to see. We asked how we could bring some peace to people in the hood. The community centre agreed to let us host a community roundtable to bring everyone together to brainstorm. We worked together and made soup and bannock. That evening, we had three questions:

What are your concerns in the community?

What would you like to see changed?

And how can you contribute to the change?

There was a lot of interaction and concern. We allowed people to use their voices, but we also encouraged people to step up. One thing was for certain, though — everyone who spoke up wanted to feel safe in our community, just like we did. An elder opened and closed the meeting.

Out of this meeting came a community patrol, which would later be called White Pony Lodge. An elder came up with the name through ceremony. Twice a week, we patrolled our community to bring a sense of safety and togetherness.

Our Twitter hashtag was #endviolenceinnorthcentral.

People walked with us and we brought joy to a community that had been overtaken by gang violence. One evening, a known gang member stopped us to tell us there were needles behind his house that he would like us to discard, and then he thanked us for what we were doing. (The irony, right?)

I was still going to church, and everyone prayed at the front of the church for me and White Pony Lodge. After the powerful prayer, another prayer warrior approached me and handed me a note. Among other things she had written the following:

> *I saw you dressed in regalia and you were leading the group as we walked. You were holding a sword*

in one hand and a lit torch in the other. My
Creator said, "You are given authority to walk the
land and help people on their healing journey. For
what you have overcome in your personal journey
you now have authority over."

This was when I started on my journey to find out who I was as an Indigenous woman. I went to my first sweat soon after. I began to heal and feel connected to my culture. My heritage had been taken from me when I was first put into foster care. Losing my culture growing up was hard and continued to affect me into my adult life. I had always tried to fit in because I didn't know who I was or how to reach this person who I longed to be. The more I grow, the more I make sense of it all.

I worked two jobs and I was a part of White Pony Lodge, which patrolled every weekend. I would patrol a few times a month and attend board meetings. I spoke with friends, ladies at work, and people who reached out on social media who were stuck in the cycles of addiction and gang life; sometimes their stories included prostitution, and my heart cried out for them. I still longed to do something to help.

I approached Defend Dignity to see if I could propose an initiative to take to our Indigenous communities to bring awareness to our Sisters and help in the fight to end sexual exploitation. Defend Dignity agreed to sponsor a pilot project called Strengthen Our Sisters (SOS). Our goal was to partner with First Nations communities for the empowerment of Indigenous women and their communities by increasing awareness of sexual exploitation and sex trafficking. A good friend of mine and I prayed and brainstormed about how to make this hope a reality.

In the spring of 2017, we held our first women's gathering in an Indigenous community in Treaty 4 Saskatchewan. The day consisted of introductions; an information session using a video developed by Defend Dignity, called, "Not in my Backyard," and other information; lunch; followed by my story and a talking circle, which was led by an elder. There were about twenty participants, including one of my daughters, Kasheena, who helped. The ages ranged from teens to sixty plus. The women were engaged and, when asked, they told me they learned what sexual exploitation was and that it was not our shame to carry. It was not the shame of our relations that are immersed in that lifestyle, but it was something that had been done to us. Our goal was to leave there with a new hope that some would step up and talk about this more and raise awareness in their own community.

I spent most of my life being shamed and berated for the things I did and often for what I didn't do. It was the surprise of my life when I learned that someone had nominated me and the Women of White Pony Lodge for the 2017 YWCA Women of Distinction Award for being change-makers in the whole city of Regina. As Jan, our nominator, and the White Pony Lodge team sat at this awards night after our first year being in the community, we felt it was a great honour to be nominated with some amazing other groups.

Earlier in the week, I'd gone to the thrift store to find a dress. I truly didn't know what to wear for such a fancy dancy occasion. I found a gold-coloured, tight-fitting dress with a broach attached. "Yes, this will do." It was a type of dress I had never worn before, but knowing everyone else was going to be dressed up nice, I wanted to fit in. Then there were the shoes. I don't wear heels, ever, but for this evening, I bought a pair of black pumps. What was I thinking? Getting dressed for this evening, I had butterflies. Looking in the mirror, I started to feel undeserving, like we weren't going to win. Why would the organizers award four Indigenous women this great honour? I couldn't even believe we had been nominated.

Driving to the event, self-doubt took over and my anxiety kicked in. Meeting up with the other ladies eased my nerves a bit, until all the nominees had to walk together to the stage, me in heels. As we walked single file, I just kept praying I wouldn't fall. (Heels and I don't get along.) As soon as we were introduced and we all headed to our tables, I peeled those pumps off. The food was fantastic — roasted chicken and salads galore, potatoes made to perfection, and piles and piles of desserts. I was in plate heaven and the company was superb.

After dinner, several other category winners were announced and the crowd applauded. Then it came to our category, Community Group Making a Difference. We ladies grabbed hands and said, "No matter what, it's an honour to be here."

All I remember is the announcer saying, "White Pony Lodge" and everyone clapping. I quickly slipped on my pumps and tried to hold back my tears as we made our way to the podium. I was amazed at being recognized for our endeavour to show love to our community and our desire to do something to make it safer. We didn't expect the recognition of our efforts or for White Pony Lodge to be plastered all over our city news or to receive a letter of congratulations from the Minister of Status of Women. Our community said what they wanted and what they longed for — to feel safe as they walked down the street. As a community, we were able to provide that sense of safety.

∞

One evening we were beginning our patrol and as we turned the corner we saw two little girls who were not any older than eight or nine.

"Are you the people that pick up needles?" one girl asked shyly.

"Yes, we are," I said gently. "Do you know where some are?"

The other little girl pointed to where there were bags of what looked like garbage in the driveway. Someone had torn some of them apart, and when we looked closer, there were hundreds of used needles and drug paraphernalia mixed in with them. Some needles had no caps. I looked at the girls and thanked them.

That's when their dad walked out of the house. "Those needles have been there for a couple of days," he said. "I'm thankful you guys are here to clean it up."

We found 50 full methadone bottles and pills that we were not sure what to do with. We called around and the fire department came out to help us dispose of it all. It was an amazing opportunity for our community to come together, starting with those little girls. We found out later that the tenant of the house had been kicked out, and the landlord had just thrown all the bags out and left them there.

The Women of Distinction Award was a gentle reminder that when people come together seeking change, much can be accomplished. As part of the award, we also received a necklace, which hangs in my room, reminding me of the care and love I have for my community. These patrols are my gift to the children that ran alongside us as we walked.

∞

I share my story of overcoming and some of my accomplishments, not to brag — no, far from it. I share them to highlight the good in my life and how I fight to survive, still to this day. I want people to know what God has done, and continues to do, in my life. I'm highly honoured that the Creator has chosen me to represent change. I'm definitely a work in progress, and even as I write this memoir, I continue to fight through my triggers, which still happen way too often. In the past, I used to deal with them by working too hard and taking too much on. I had it in my head that I had to do everything and anything that was asked of me. I've learned that that was not true. I know this now. Some days, I'm in a dark place, not able to see the light. Those days are hard, but they're not as bad now that I've learned to deliberately deal with my past traumas.

I believe there's a reason for everything. I believe that no matter what I went through, I have a story, and my story is like those of so many of my Indigenous brothers and sisters. It's the story of rejection and deceit. It's the story of abuse and shame. It's the story that many of my friends, family members, and my beautiful mom were never able to tell because their lives were cut short. I tell my story so that people can watch out for women and young girls who are being exploited. They're not exploited because they choose to be. They're there because life dealt them a bad hand.

I have a deep desire and burden to help women who are where I've been. I want to help them know they can live a free life.

∞

When I woke up, the smell of sweetgrass and sage still scented my nose. I had taken the families and youth that I worked with at Indigenous Christian Fellowship to the feast and Round Dance at the First Nations University of Canada. We had a time to remember. We all piled into the white, fifteen-passenger van. The children laughed and buckled their seat belts, this time with no fussing. They must have been excited too. I have such a bad sense of direction. I kept asking one of the passengers if I was going the right way.

She laughed and asked, "How long did you go to the university? You'd think you'd know your way."

I looked at her in the rear-view mirror and said, "Don't make me turn this van around." We all broke out into laughter.

Once we made it to our destination, we all piled out of the van, feast supplies in hand. The girls and ladies wore ribbon skirts as a sign of respect for our culture. My skirt was blue with flowers and three ribbons on the bottom: one yellow, one green, one blue. It was cold outside. The wind was brisk and blowing, so we all hustled into the building. The sweetgrass and sage aroma let us know we were in the right place. We shared food and held hands and danced in a circle. Children laughed and adults joined in. I smile, remembering the fun I experienced. It was a beautiful time of togetherness in sobriety that warmed the soul. The drums beat to the sound of my heart. Listening to the drums calms me and restores my own natural rhythm. I love learning about my culture.

∞

I ended up getting sick with a gallbladder infection and had to get it removed. A couple of months later, my kidney stones were acting up and I had to have surgery to have them broken down. After my surgery, I got a blood infection and was very sick. I was given a couple weeks off work to get better, but it didn't feel long enough. I'd hit a breaking point where I felt like my whole world was in turmoil. Depression and anxiety came and went. One day, I'd wake up and be calm, and another day, I'd wake up and wonder what the hell was going on. Something had to change.

That day, I wrote a resignation letter at 12 a.m. and sent it at 12:30 am. I was not in the right mindset to make such a rash decision, and when I woke up, I immediately regretted sending it. *What was I thinking? How am I going to pay my bills?* My heart felt so broken and I couldn't figure it out. There were so many reasons for this decision, but even so, I didn't feel like a sane person would have resigned without thinking it through.

I went to the doctor and he prescribed antidepressants. *Should I take the pills? It will not make me weak.* I had to believe that in order to take that first pill. However, I decided not to take them. My biggest excuse for not taking them was weight gain, but I felt myself slowly falling back into sadness, knowing I would go to work the next day.

My mental health has been attacked for most of my life. I have been depressed since I was a little girl. And, right from my earliest memories, I have always heard, "What's wrong with you?" or "There's something wrong with her." I think about the times I sat alone and quiet for hours under the hot blazing sun, picking weeds right to the smallest one, just to make it look like I was doing something. Then there were the days I sat in the rankest bars, looking for a mark or looking for a fight because I needed to keep myself medicated with drugs and alcohol and keep my adrenaline hyped. I was always ready to fight, but inside I was so sad.

I don't want to hit low places anymore. I want to be freed from that burden. Sometimes, I am in such a great place in life and accomplish so much. And I don't realize that, it doesn't mean that I was always in a good state of mind. I could actually be in my manic place. But when people see all the good works I do, they don't look at me as being manic — they look at me as accomplished. This puts pressure on me. I would like people to see me as a whole person.

As I write these words, my heart is beating so hard. I desperately want to gain a better understanding of how to deal with my emotions. When I think back on my healing journey, I ask, when were my good days? I can think of good times or breakthroughs, but when were my actual good days? It sounds harsh, when this book is to be a "helping tool" to those who find themselves where I once was.

I suppose I should look deeper. I have come so far and I should be humbly proud of where I am today. It's not pure luck — it's by the grace of God that I'm even writing my book, a dream I've had since I was a little girl, writing in my journal, my binder full of hope and love poems. A longing love, the beauty of the full yellow flower to the princess needing love.

It is time for me to retrain my mind not to see so much failure or even to look at my mental health as a failure. I'm here today against all odds. I should look at what has happened to me as my gifts instead of the labels that were cast on me and embedded in my mind.

There's so much hope, probably even more hope than I'm aware of, because I feel it. I feel a breakthrough fast approaching — a shift in the way I see myself, the way I react. I breathe deeply. Slow and steady. Motivation is the key — when I'm motivated, I get things done. Growing spiritually helps me emotionally. I love working out. I love the sweat pouring off me after a Crossfit session. I love the feeling of sore stomach muscles the day after a good workout. I love eating healthy food, doing meal prep, making Kombucha smoothies in the mornings, knowing they fuel my body. I love going for long jogs, running out of breath from pushing myself to jog those two extra blocks, bent over gasping for breath, knowing I still have two kilometres to go. The feeling of accomplishment after jogging five kilometres, even on the treadmill. I love being in a sweat, feeling close to my culture. I love when I am looking after my holistic self.

I can't forget the sun is shining more, now that the weather has improved, and I love the feeling when I close my eyes and face the sun. I feel its beautiful heat on my face. It brings warmth right to my soul. Oh, days ahead are beautiful indeed — a breathtaking view of my future also warms my heart. For now, it's okay to put Beatrice first. No one's going to be mad. People will understand.

I say thank you, Creator, for the image of hope. I know that my heart beating hard is not anxiety in a bad way — it's actually excitement for this evening, when we are going for a walk around Wascana Lake. The wind is blowing. It was going to be my excuse not to go, but now, I will think of the wind as a cleansing. Now I look forward to going.

From the time I was a young child to the time I spent hanging in the dark and glow of downtown, missing front teeth, bros and sis's in miniskirts, ripped stockings, and overly revealing tops, to the time visiting my children in the social worker's office, not knowing when I would have my children home, feeling lost and alone and terrified for my future, I have always said there's a reason why you have experienced all you have, and it hasn't been for nothing. I'm still alive, so I hold on to that truth.

I never expected to be where I am today. Although I'm not perfect to all, I am perfectly okay. I accept my flaws and failures. With every discovery, I grow. Sometimes, a breakthrough looks like a failure, but the Creator's grace and mercy turns it into something beautiful. As long as I don't fall victim and lose myself once and for all, as long as I seek truth and healing and jump back up when I fall, God uses my story, my compassion, and my strength to make my life a million times better and bring hope to all who hear my story. What a beautiful concept, knowing God is using my broken past and healing.

∞

In the summer of 2018, I started working for Soul's Harbour once again, this time in Shayil Home, a women's addiction home. I love my job and it has opened my eyes and my heart to that Ranch for sexually exploited women, that vision that the Creator gave me so many years ago. I see the need. I see how my sisters are hurting. I see how much I've changed. I want to offer them hope. I'm not who I used to be and although I am constantly working on myself, it's okay — we are not perfect until we get to heaven, right? None of us is, and I hold on to the hope that I'm given.

∞

I attended a conference called Soul Care, and in the year leading up to it, I did some major self-care and healing in the deep places I'd been scared to go, places that had held me in bondage. I let go of the shame and held on to the truth that the abuse was inflicted on me. I didn't ask for the abuse or the damage it did to me. I walked away from the conference after giving up my hate and anger to the Creator and asking to be shown healthy self-management. Then, I went to counselling to work through my past. There's nothing wrong with that, and while I wished I had done it ten years ago, it's all in God's timing.

I didn't write about my children's lives much in this book. They each have a story to tell, but it's up to them to share it. I want to honour their stories. I will say I'm so proud of each of them and the amazing ways they have overcome their own struggles in their lives. There's no way I could have lived this life and not have it affect them negatively. My heart breaks, thinking about that, but I'm so thankful that they have forgiven me for my part in it. It doesn't mean that it's forgotten, because that's a far cry from the truth, but I try my best and I know my children know I love them.

As parents, we can't continue to beat ourselves up for our past — even though some days it's hard — because we are not being helpful to our children when we do. We need to continue to work on our healing journey so we can be an example. I want to be an inspiration to my children because they inspire me daily.

Back in my early days as a Christian, I prayed my simple prayer for my children to stay in school until they graduated Grade 12, to never have to live on the streets or experience sexual exploitation or live in gangs, and, to this day, all of them have fulfilled this prayer request. Now, that is a miracle in itself. My children are all grown and making amazing lives for themselves.

∞

I know others who have experienced similar circumstances to mine and who struggle with a lack of hope and believe it's hard to change, but the changes they make will be worth it. With every ounce of my being, I say that my life is so much better today than it has ever been. Do I wish I could have understood everything then that I do now? Heck, yeah! It would have saved me many years of challenges and heartaches. Do I regret my walk thus far? Heck, no! Because I'm still learning and I'm still growing. As imperfect as I am, I'm perfect in God's eyes, and truly for me, that is all that matters. I'll continue to fail and sometimes stumble.

I have so much support in my life, and all I have to do is reach out. I have a loving family that stood by me through all my years of troubles and growth. My children and grandchildren are my life and my world. They know I'm not perfect, and they do not expect perfection from me. I was saved from a life that destroyed many and just about killed me many times over. And I found the Creator, who has been there for me all these years.

The encouragement I love to give is that no matter what you've been through, no matter what you've done, there is a purpose for your life. You were created for so much more than our little minds understand. We can't even comprehend God's love for us or our purpose. Those in this world who are evil will have us believe differently. But don't! Hold on to the truth that you are loved and you are valuable. No matter the colour of your skin, no matter the past you have endured, you are the Creator's idea. Now, how can we not want to honour that, with everything that we have and do!

∞

As I walk through the field, I feel the frost melt in between my cold painted toes, in my open-toed shoes. I feel the heat melting the dew in the autumn grass. As I trust in the Creator's process, it's getting much easier. Not only my feet are warmed but also my heart, with every passing step. The sun glazes through change, unforgettable change.

I'm thankful for the journey. My destination is in sight. One step at a time. My journey is just beginning. There's no more fight. I'm grateful for my black, soaked sandals as I make it to this destination. It's scary as wounds heal, but I'm thankful to the Creator for this second chance. I dare not compare. Thank you, Creator, for my life and the days I have left to explore.

Chilled to the bone,
walking home,
early morn.
Sun rises,
kisses my face,
weather changes,
Creator's amazing grace.

ACKNOWLEDGEMENTS

When I decided to write and publish my story, I had no idea what was involved in the process. Good thing or I might have changed my mind. It's not pure luck — it's by the grace of God that I've written my book, a dream I've had since I was a little girl, writing in my journal, my binder full of hope and love poems.

I'm grateful for the loving care and support I received from a number of people. Glendyne Gerrard, Director of Defend Dignity, got behind me and delved into her resources to help me write, beta read, edit, proofread, publish and market *Wolf Woman: A Search for Identity*.

I am also thankful for Lynda Allison for walking and guiding me every step of the way from the thoughts of the book to the book being in my hands. She helped me more than she will ever know.

I appreciate Lauryl Chamberlain who typed my first draft. Thank you to Becky Bradbury, Aaron Gerrard, Shalene Gerrard, Jennifer Lucking and Katelynn Robertson for Beta reading my draft. Shalene Gerrard, Jennifer Lucking, Judy Whaling, and Brock Tyler proofread the final text. I appreciate Sherry Hinman's approach to editing, keeping in mind the importance of preserving the author's voice. Laura Dieter Fauchon took my vision and created the book illustration and Kheyla Pehlke designed the book cover.

I'm proud of my children who managed to give me space to write. My Creator shone bright on me throughout my life changes and the writing of this book.

Now I'm holding my memoir in my hand, glad I've undertaken this journey to share my life story with you.

Manufactured by Amazon.ca
Bolton, ON